BURIED TALENTS

By Terry Atkinson

An exposition of the Character, Talents,
and Book of Jonah

NEW LIVING PUBLISHERS

164 Radcliffe New Road, Whitefield, Manchester M45 7TU England

www.newlivingpublishers.co.uk

First published 2000

British Library Cataloguing in Publication Data
A catalogue record for this book is available
from the British Library.

ISBN 1 899721 03 7

Scripture quotations are from the King James Version
of the Bible unless otherwise stated.

Cover design: Greg Clifton

Produced and printed in England for
NEW LIVING PUBLISHERS
164 Radcliffe New Road, Whitefield, Manchester M45 7TU by

by:

MOORLEY'S Print & Publishing
23 Park Rd., Ilkeston, Derbys DE7 5DA
Tel/Fax: (0115) 932 0643

This book is dedicated to all those Believers who think they possess no talents, with the prayer that they might discover just how many they have, and use them to the glory of God.

CONTENTS

CHAPTER 1

Introduction

There are very few people you meet in the slide and the skid of life who will claim to have great talents. Most are so self effacing, that they have no face at all. They don't recognise what is given to them because they sometimes see men walking as trees.[1] They say they have such few talents, they are not worth bothering about. These very people, the mixed and the mixed up multitude, will only ever see Jonah as a runaway. Nothing more than the facts as revealed, that he tried to run away from God. What they miss by a wide margin, is the fact that some twenty-five talents can be clearly seen and marked out in his life. As we read of this man of God the eyes of our understanding and heart need to be opened wide. As you read the book of Jonah, and 'buried talents' you will read it and see it as you have never read it or seen it presented before, you will discover that all your gifts are in Him. The book that you thought was so dull suddenly becomes alive as if new life has been breathed into it from the mouth of God. We can take the same journey as he did, to the bottom of the sea. Within the realms of the unexpected you will witness the unexpected and find that this man has been sent to preach to you in the quiet corner of your heart. There is the voice of John the Baptist in this book crying still 'Prepare you the way of the Lord.'[2] Let those mountains be removed and let every valley be filled until the glory of the Lord fills your heart and life as the waters cover the sea.

There are those whom we feel have a fistful of God-given abilities, while we have but one item only. When they were being granted we were 'short changed.' Even the coinage we have received in our deposit has no king's head on one side, and the other side is but blank. The person with one talent can accomplish far more if that given can be taken and used by God. There is no lack in God, and He has said that we shall lack no good thing. After giving all we have, small or great, it is God who adds value to it, as he adds value even to sparrows. The power of the one talent is in the surrender of it. With God, the one becomes many, without God, the many can never be the full designation of what might have been. When we surrender the small, there is a greater power to develop it into something tall. That surrendered as weak is made strong.

That with no relevance at all is made to matter because it is a matter of God's honour that is involved. Out of nothing He makes everything. He can make something out of nothing if you are that nothing.

There are so many gifted people, who don't use what they already have. God is waiting for them to use the gifts already given and received, and when they do, they make way for new things and much more. During the feeding of the Five Thousand, as pieces of bread were taken, more appeared as other pieces disappeared. Even that which they have, is lost to the area of its use. That talent can slip from our fingers as a ring from a thin finger or the axe head from the shaft. It can have been part of you for so long that it has lost its song. The years can mask it so that it is no longer recognised. There is no appeal in it. That has become part of the acceptance of what we think we are, and not where we are. The years can glaze your eyes to what you have and what you can be in the Kingdom of God. There can be that deliberate running away, and playing hide and seek with God as both Adam and Jonah did. The Creator goes to great creative and caring acts to find us wherever we are, and God doesn't always unearth that buried with a spade. He can and does use wind, whales, worms - all found in the book of Jonah, yet, so used as to discover where we are in the deepest depths or even under the ocean. When we reach the mud at the bottom of the sea we will still find Jehovah drawing plans in that black slime of what He intends for us. We only ever see the straw that the Children of Israel made bricks from.[3] We never see or notice that produced in brick form. The furnace we see, the brick kiln, the field from which the straw was gathered but we fail to see the end product of all the hard work. These bricks were to build pyramids, and that granted to you can be used to build an Everlasting Kingdom that houses no dead Pharaoh but a living Christ. The bottom of that ocean becomes the very hand of God to lift us back into life, and put that back into circulation and operating in what the Master created us for. Each wave becomes a helping hand. All things are made to symphonise together as an orchestra to those who love God. Romans 8:28.

There are those who think to bury their talents is a matter of digging a hole in the ground, and covering them up never to be resurrected, or tying them to a stone and throwing them into the deepest part of the sea.

A talent can be buried by some attitude. There can be the feeling of the whip on the spirit as we are discouraged. There can be the petty anger, so petty, that is less than petty cash. It can flare up and leave that which promises so much as a burned cinder. From it, as He blows upon the smoking flax, Cinderella can step forth so well dressed and ready to serve alongside the Young Prince of Glory. There can be that feeling, developing into a doctrine within your heart that you are just not good enough. Pity is bad, self-pity is worse. That pity of self can shut the door to every opportunity presented to us as it did with Jonah. How much like us all he is! We read of him in this book and we see him in some very awkward corners, but as he comes around every corner and goes over every wave, God is there. We manage sometimes to become the awkward in that awkward situation. He is never left lost, feeling that he was born a speckled bird, or a bird with only one wing and foot flying nowhere and going in the same direction when walking. That given to us by God for His work can be lost in the comparison of what you have with another. They are the fruit, you are the branch. They are the singing voice you are the hum or the whistle. Soon an inferiority complex can make the experience far more complex than it was ever meant to be. Who would compare a screech with a song? There can be, as it was at the beginning with Jonah, the open rebellion against God. All these things are the very grounds that we bury them under. That meant to be used openly is caged and treated as some pet parrot, when it should have such rarity and beauty to display for its creator.

Making you different in your realm can be lost in circumstances as the coin was lost in the home in Luke 15. The years may add concrete to the burial place, and where we lost it, but God is there, and seeks to bring us back to our abilities for accomplishment. Right can become ruin, and that given can be wasted as a fortune, the trinkets of life replacing them. The surgeon's scalpel can be used for spreading butter, rather than lancing the lifeless form. God reads the epitaph of long standing which is placed where everything is hidden which should be revealed. As resurrection is written on the leaf of every tree, so where your talent lies there is a constant echo coming from it to be lifted and dusted down, and clothed in acceptance to be used again. You can bury what God intended you to have and work at among your circle of activity. Life, like a huge stone can be placed over the mouth, and conceal the ability. The deafness of the deaf and the dumbness of the dumb when we turn aside, can be part of that created for expression. There can be that vow of the heart, rashly spoken, 'I will never do that again', and this becomes your skull and crossbones, signifying the pirate you have become. That fleshly and fat suddenly becomes less than skin and bone. The shape is there, but the substance is missing. Many just lay their talents on one side, and they become as the rusty plough blade, when it should be shining clean through much use. The parable of the blade that shone and the blade that was rusty is the parable of your life. One was shining and beaming through the constant cleaning of rubbing along the furrows, striking stone and rock. The other had the wind blowing upon it and the wind beating it mercilessly until it lost its glow and a red flush formed a coat upon it. One looked like a medal and a moonbeam while the other looked like a fallen rusty leaf from a tree and a slipped chopping edge. History is so eloquent with a silver tongue telling its own story of those who might have accomplished much for God. As it speaks, it tells, and as it tells it sighs and sobs between the tears for the children of Rachel who are not.[4] Children brought to birth at so great cost, but fail to mature into the measureless.

Jonah is presented to us in both the Old and the New Testaments, so that all might have hope. You can rise with him, you can stand, walking and talking with him in a rediscovered ability of accessibility. The book of Jonah is Jonah's book, and it becomes a schoolroom and schoolmaster with tests and passes. There is light shed from the book as some illuminating force. It is the light, brighter than the shining of the noonday sun or the pure light of a long day. In it we can see the one who lived with a concealed talent. The re-discovery of spirituality will see it fully restored and seated on a throne. God never gives up; He never buries His abilities when seeking you. There is no grace gift, which is hidden when you hide. The arm and the hand are not squeezed into a small gift when He seeks you. It may be a long time and a long walk but He arrives at the end. Then comes the moment waited for like some promised holiday or birthday. The years are lifted back. The veil between you and Him is parted and He steps in and all becomes today that was yesterday. His love is deeper than burial, and it is further reaching than resurrection. It is wider than the separating years. It continues longer than nations. God is not buried with your burying. You cannot place under earth that exalted far above the heavens, having authority, dominion, thrones and power. His arm of love is not short so that it becomes a stump half buried, without roots, or that, which doesn't bear fruit. The heart, which loves cares and seeks, is never cold, but always bold and beckoning.

Life is as many hands, which snatch and take from us, life, which can break the strong ties; it can tear away the anchor marooning you in some situation that you never intended to be. In that island is buried treasure. That intended to express all the glory of God becomes just a dim echo of the full tone. Jesus sells all to buy the land and claim the treasure covered up in it. He seeks it like a Merchant looking for goodly pearls. The price He paid for it was the blood and ransom He gave when dying on a cross. Dying but rising again with it. Taking captivity captive and obtaining gifts for men. The disarmed are fully armed for accomplishment again. They now have a more enduring substance. Rescued and reinstated by Jesus Christ.

When talents are buried, it is not as if this suddenly happens. It is a slide and a nudge; step by step we enter into that darkness which acts as some shroud to surround our abilities. The real you, still dressed in modern tailoring becomes but dummy and scarecrow for the real thing. There is less use of the thing, then even less, until that which should have been as sunshine turns into blackest night, and a miracle has been reversed. Sometimes, there is that false humility, which tells you that God could never really use you, and so you never give him a chance. We all follow the echoes of our own hearts but we treat that hollow noise as if it is the real thing. We go where the light from our own hearts directs us, but, sometimes, we walk into that which covers and clouds. There is the possibility of becoming half-informed and half-formed, never reaching the full circle of capability or the outer circumference of what we really are. You may throw it all away, but God has a way of bringing it back 'with usury', for there is something elastic about what God has placed in your heart. It is tied to His heart. There is a place where grief and hurt raises its monument to what might have been. Within the feelings of pain, the achievement is crushed into another form of pain. Talents are buried deeply in pain, and it takes the One who suffered more than you to release you from it, and that takes healing and releasing power, but have no doubt, because the very word salvation[5] suggests healing, restoring and releasing. You can get out of the routine of using what you have for God, so that which once brought joy brings no peace. That which inspired and exhilarated you only leaves you as dumb! There are no museums for talent lost and found. They are yours; they both die and live with you, side by side as twins and brothers. Abilities live as you live. They are free and full expressions of what you are, and your best moments, which are your happiest.

The list is endless, or should I say the hole is very deep, and the granules, which cover our usefulness, are many. Our usefulness in taken into the realm of that not used or useable. This place of that unused is as a deep pit, and no one has anything to draw them up. Their burial is as that lost. So low, even the depth of the unseen can't find us. David had the same thing in mind in Psalm 55:6, when he wished for the wings of a dove that he might fly away and be at rest. God didn't answer that prayer. He left him there, and he began to write. The King of Israel did not put his pen away or break it; he simply dipped it into his experience and wrote to bless others.[6] It takes the Christ who arose from the dead to arise again in your heart, and as He arises, He brings a new Gospel of restoration with Him. He puts that back into place and you back into shape. The orchestra and the conductor, the fiddle and the bow are together again making happy music, and all are enlivened, enriched and blessed. The soul is lifted, the blackness is taken away, and there is the deep penetration of the Sun Of Righteousness, risen with healing in His wings.[7] The cold, naked and desolate are bathed in a new light. The talent lost, is found. The talent buried is unearthed. The cutting edge is restored; the field in which the treasure was buried is bought and that which can be used unearthed, every measure of earth contained some new thing. This is why Jesus went into the tomb. That not used for many years is brought into its own again. It is the revival of restoration.

Talents, which are God-given, God-created and God-inspired, move through the whole realm of human activity and achievement. We are thinking of those specific activities used to promote the glory of God. To each one a finger of God is loaned. We have borrowed what we have that we might return it to the Lender, broader, bigger and that added which makes the entire better for it being lent to us. The empty hand is returned full. When the talents were given in the parables in Matthew 25, they were given to 'every man' 'each according to his ability'.[8] There is ability for everyone as a token of God's grace deposited as treasure within a vessel of clay. Yours might be in painting, sculpturing, moulding, whistling, singing, leading, or preaching. The list is endless because the talents are so many. Each army is not all weapons. Weapons, as talents are only part of the whole.

The meaning of the word talent is found in the Greek word 'talanton', a weight, and a coin, to spend and be spent. True to the monarch's image. The image and superscription of God is on that capacity. It does mean a full measure, a full expression of that which you do. If it is that adding weight and dimension how do you weigh in God's scales? How large hearted are you? How much have you grown? There is no corner cut, there are no parts buried, none is withheld when it is being used for the purpose it was designed. The thought is that adding value to us. Glory is that adding weight. Each talent is a deposit of God's abilities and nature. Variety and abundance are part of it. Originally the word talent meant a 'balance' the perfect equation, the perfect equilibrium. You are most balanced when blessed in your work for God. In the receiving and the using of your talent, you have that balancing you, giving you a perfect poise of ballerina quality. In the Old Testament, Dr Young [9] gives the word talent, found in Exodus 25:39, as that meaning a 'circular cake'. It is from this cake and your ability that the three thousand and the five thousand will be fed even though you see your gifting as five small loaves and two small fish. Many will be blessed by it if it is not hidden or denied, and not attributed to other sources rather than God, the fountain of all ability. God can and you can. The pot may be nothing, but there is enough in it to pay the creditors and bring glory to God, 2 Kings 4. In the Old Testament, from the talent there were 3,000 shekels from that one source. Can you measure what God can do through your ability? Ability is stability until accomplishment. Even a tree or rose bush has some sort of talent through which to express nature, light and colour. It is of little use declaring in despair that we have no talent. When we do, we bury it as much as that shut up in a glass case, or taken and buried in Davy Jones' Locker. Our English words 'gift' and 'ability' come from the Greek word 'talent'.

There is no-one in the whole of Scripture that illustrates the burying of the talents which you have more than the Prophet Jonah. All the parables of Jesus based on buried talents, and those who turn their backs on what should be before them is fully illustrated through the prophet's life. Jesus was always trying to get people to develop. Whatever you are; be a good one.

This book will take you step by step through the life and activities of Jonah, bringing you back to the place of the talent being used, and the Giver being glorified. Until every note or every word, every page or every tool tells its own finishing story. Jonah will give you hope as no other. There are those who partially buried their talents for a time. Jonah does a complete work; he buried his preaching and persuading ability into the belly of a whale after being in the side of a ship. It is a downward path he treads, but God walks down with him to bring him up again.

You might possess the greatest of talents, but a 'Stradivarius' is only as a plyboard instrument unless it is used. Paganini and his one-stringed violin are of less use than one made out of cardboard unless it is taken up and used. The ability of the person must be set free to express itself just as much as a bird uses its wings, a man well used by God, means that God is on the throne, and there is the possibility of every knee bowing before Him, even the knees of Jonah.

Get the facts straight, no-one could preach or teach like Jonah under prophetic inspiration, but the water of the sea drowned his ability, and the east wind blew him towards his destiny and calling. Even a worm gnawed away at what should have brought much comfort to him. The Juniper tree served its purpose.[10] When we run in the opposite direction to where God has told us to go, we bury our talent. We commence paying our own fare when we bury the very thing, which would take us to our destination. While others pray and row as they did in the book of Jonah, we sleep with our gifting lost in our pyjamas and wrapped up in the bed blankets, sleeping with us.

In the book of Jonah we find the sea where the talent sails not. There is a whole country wherein lies buried every shape and form, which God expects of the believer. By the grace of God, this book will resurrect that within you, and put it back into circulation doing what it should do, and bringing blessing to many people.

Notes

1   Mark 8:24
2   Matthew 3:3
3   Exodus 5:7,7,10,11,
      12,13,15,16,18
4   Matthew 2:18

5   Acts 4:12
6   Psalm 45:1
7   Malachi 4:2
8   Matthew 25:15

9   Robert Young's
      Analytical Concordance
      of the Bible. Published
      by Lutterworth Press.
10 Jonah 4:6,7

CHAPTER 2

The One who has every talent

There is an antidote to Jonah and those peculiar idiosyncrasies which we have, and they are found in the New Testament phrase 'A greater than Jonah is here'.[1] Jesus was greater not only in comparison but also in substance, and in the way He allowed himself to be used by God. He never was on a foreign mission. He came unto His own and they didn't receive Him. He was in prison and they didn't visit Him. He was hungry and they did not feed Him. When He came to die He was not paying His own fare as Jonah did. When He died He shed His blood for the sins of others not His own. Jesus became one of us so that He might influence us better. Then, we might take what He offers to us in talent form, and trade with it until we make a success and the success makes us.

The contrast between Jonah and Jesus

For the Jonah journeys we have the gems and jottings of Jesus as recorded in the Gospels and the Epistles. When commencing anything, we make a start with That greater than our abilities and that is what Jesus Christ is. If I would have a part, then I must come to the fullness of it all. There is no unwilling message of the messenger in the Lord Jesus Christ. As the young artist sits at the feet of the great artist, or makes sketches from a masterpiece, we would contemplate Jesus Christ and all of His talents, revealing how to use them, and how to be used by God. Just as Paul sat at the feet of Gamaliel the Jewish teacher, we would sit at His feet and be joined by adoring Mary with her alabaster vase of ointment.[2] He set His face as a flint, and He could say 'The zeal of your house has eaten me up,'[3] that zeal has eaten into my soul. Jesus unearthed talents in the most unsuspecting places. He adds dignity to men. He makes you believe in men.

Jonah, as a prophet, was unique in that he was raised up as a Jew to go to a Gentile nation, those housed in the city of Nineveh. The mission of Jesus was to the whole world. What was partial and fragmented in Jonah was the full in Jesus Christ. The world was the parish of Jesus. The book of Hebrews speaks of the world as His house that He has built, and people like Jonah and Moses were only servants, as also were the angelic

13

bands.[4] For the one talent in one man, Jonah, we have every talent in Christ. The presence of God did not go with Jesus Christ, He is that presence. He was the fullness of the Godhead bodily.[5] He did not have to hide. When they tried to bury him, He arose bringing so many things with Him. Where and when Jonah stopped short, Jesus went all the way. He was the Way,[6] He was the Truth, not part of it or some single thought. There was nothing breaking up in Him, as the ship was ready to break. He set His face as a flint.[7] Jesus wasn't a spark to light the fire; He was the fire and created the spark and the sparkle. This servant went into the city he was sent to, but Jonah went around in a decreasing circle, when he disobeyed. He was that good and wholesome thing sent to help all those who fall short. He wasn't simply the voice beckoning us on, but the person stood beside us helping us along. There was only the sleep of the exhausted for Him, but when He awoke the storm went to sleep. The waves threw their crowns at His feet. He turned them into slabs for walking on. Jesus, as Jonah, saw His teaching work, building bridges and spanning gulfs.

Jesus was faithful in all things

From His faithfulness, we can take faithfulness, for there is nothing covering it, and find Him as our prime example of what every talented person should do with His talent. The captain of the ship that Jonah paid his fare to is long dead. The fare has been spent. However, that committed to Jesus, He is able to keep until that Eternal Day. Jesus lives on, in the power of a resurrected life.

The Lord's Christ never went on a ship that was out of control. The storms never put fear into Him, but He put peace into the raging sea. He put a smile on its face! Jesus didn't descend into the sea to be buried with His God-given ability. No; He stilled the storm-tossed sea,[8] so that which He had, those miraculous talents could be displayed as He walked on water, the very element which would have destroyed any and every part of that found in Jonah, and all who live like him in rebellion. Jesus used the storm to exhibit what He was. It was a stage not for sinking but for preaching and displaying His miraculous powers of achieving things against all the odds. When the odds were stacked against Him, He never thought it was odd. His actions spoke louder than words - His words were actions. Jesus didn't have to be thrown into the sea. He threw the word of God into the situation and saw its miracle proportions. Wonder of wonders He didn't even offer a religious prayer as every crewmember did on the ship that Jonah journeyed on. The ship carried Him. The Christ carried the ship and every ship. Destiny was not His master; He was the master of it. The reins were in His hands; He wasn't clinging to the wheel of something running away into hell. The captain of the ship had to do his work, and he did it to the best of his ability. Jesus was the Captain of the whale, wind and waves. Everything would fit into the hollow of His hand. The radiance of every moment fits neatly into His smiling face. They cast lots that the runaway might be thrown into the sea as oil to calm it. They cast lots for Jesus that He might redeem the world and bring the Jehovah of Peace into full view, for He was the face of God, John 14:8. The word 'suffice' means 'enough'.

Jesus retained His ministry while being in hell itself, 1 Peter 3:19. He never let go the purpose for which God had called Him. There was that in the character of Jesus, the deepest and vilest sea could not wash out. No wave of opposition could bowl Him overboard. Those talents were not thrown overboard or washed overboard. There was many a time when the Whale would have swallowed them up, but He was more than a conqueror. Here is the man, so talented that He speaks and fish come to line and hook. We don't even know if there was any bait on the end of the line, Matthew 17:27, where it says only a hook was thrown into the sea.

Jesus delighted to do all things

In His ministry, there was no sleep while sailors perished. Jesus himself drew near.[9] There was that part of His heart, which could never be broken off, or would ever, be surrendered to the god of sea, earth or sky. From His heart given to God came all the things He was. One of the hallmarks of the gifting of Jesus was that He always delighted to do God's will.[10] He always inclined towards it as a tree to water. There were no days with great yawning gaps in them. He was ever as the full bucket. There was no dark night and despondent days where He was drifting into oblivion - He kept cool because He was cool.

Looking unto Jesus can save you such a lot of pain. He is still the loaves and the fishes to be divided by the disciples among many. All are filled as they feed on Him. We don't read about the malingering prophet sharing his food with anyone. We do read that he became a feast for the hungry fish.

There can be that place of 'Bypass Meadows', so illustrated in Pilgrim's Progress,[11] which can be avoided, by learning from the son of Amittai, the second name of Jonah, Jonah 1:1

Jesus had a capacity for dealing with every character

Jesus had a capacity for every character. He is the whole and you are the part. God never intended you to be as God. The notice on the Minster's vestry door said 'Remember that you are not God!' Another declaration said 'You are son and I am Father.' Simply being a light reflector, letting what He is become what you are. If you can't be a torch of light then hold one to show others the way. While you are illuminating their way you will be illuminating your own. Simply expressing and reflecting all that Jesus Christ stood for. I may not have what I want, but I can be what He makes me. The first words of the returning prodigal in Luke 15, were 'Father, make me' There may be just a few talents in your heart, but one of them may be to take the master's shoes off, and place them on his feet again. There are those who have to feed the donkeys. Who will pour the water before he washes the feet? What can Simon of Cyrene do? He can carry the cross. Your expressions of service are what you accomplish the best. What you aren't so good at, leave that with God to develop. Maybe the time isn't right now. The cows will come home just as sure as the ships will sail in. Look unto Jesus until that is perfect, matured in you. Talents abound in the New Testament, found in people who would make no great claim to fame. Everything we have, everything we do, every expression of service should be a reflection of Jesus Christ. I cannot be the naked flame, but I can be the light from that flame. To be something is to do something. Jesus never had to be what He wasn't called to be. Neither was Jonah. Neither are you.

Many were involved in small ways in the ministry of Jesus

'The women ministered to Him of their substance.'[12] 'Substance' meaning 'the things that are.' Joseph of Arimathea lent his tomb.[13] There was a small boy who gave loaves and fishes.[14] The house at Bethany was given. Dorcas gave her needle. Lydia sold and bought dyes. There was a woman who broke open an alabaster box of ointment. God was at hand seeking to add something to Jonah throughout is mission, but he closed the door. There were those who lent their donkey and provided an Upper Room. Why did they do these things? The shadow of the Almighty fell across their paths. These were what they considered their talents should be used for, when they were given back to the Giver. Jesus always made that bigger and better, which was brought to Him. The One with so many gifts at His calling worked, and went in and out among them. He did something to them. What the potter may do to the clay, Jesus Christ did to these. He placed perfume in the clay. He found them as clay in the ditch not having been manipulated by the skill of the potter, but left them studded with jewels of inexpressible worth. As His hand was placed upon them, what was in that hand became part of them. He added something to them, because He adopted as His motto 'The night will come when no man may work'.[15] Jonah could have matured much earlier if he had yielded as that surrendered.

It is not more of His talents we need to receive, but obedience in the rarities we already possess. It isn't more seeds we require to have a greater harvest, but it is the planting of the ones we already possess. It is not a matter of having more, but using fully what is ours, and as we do we copy Christ. You become a 'copy cat'. If Jesus had only one talent it would have been so used that all the music would have gone from the trumpet to cheer and enliven others. The entire scent would have been used from the flower. Such was his expressed purpose and devotion. What He did with one capacity, He did with all. We can't use an armoury until we learn to use one sword. In giving yourself, give yourself to the one thing that you might achieve many things.

Jesus was fully armed and equipped

Jesus couldn't be less than all men; He had to be more. His equipment was complete. He will always be as the one fully armed, armed to the teeth. That was granted Him, and He used it to establish the glory of God in the Kingdom of God. All that Jonah required was granted by God. He found himself as a beggar, because he refused the true riches of grace which takes us to the goals required. The Psalmist, referring to the heritage of the Lord had said 'Blessed is the man who has his quiver full'.[16] The quiver of Jesus was full, and He appeared as a man ready for action. He used His talents as a Bowman would use arrows or a warrior his weapons. Jonah breaks the bow and misses the target through going for something smaller. We aim for what our heart is - large or small! Graces abounded in Him, and His life's work was the unearthing of talents in the lives of others. He was the wise man that built His house on the rock. When He was digging deep, He unearthed so much potential in others. Every time He spoke, He was digging. Every time He journeyed, He was on a mission to discover new worlds in old planets. Those planets were the pulverised lives of people. If the eye was blind, he restored it. If the music had ceased, he brought it to life again. If the ability had turned into vulnerability, He dealt with that in the same manner. Jesus didn't just take a gift from a man; He simply restored it and put it to good use. Why go on a detour with a runaway servant, and delay what God requires for ten or twenty years? He is the Lord of the 'now'.

Jesus saw the potential in people

Matthew was good with finance; Jesus took that and blessed it. He had the ability to see the potential in men, as He did with Nathaniel in John 1:47-50, the man He saw under the tree in whom there was no guile, no bait. Those good at catching fish; He used His abilities to teach them to catch men. Jesus only saw and released this potential because He was a man of like passions. He wanted to serve God. All his faculties were brought into every event. He turned disappointments into appointments. Those with empty hearts, He took what He had and placed into them such a fullness. All this was contained in the message of Jonah when Nineveh repented. It is repentance which opens the opportunities to our talents.

Jesus wasn't a square, He was all round, providing an 'all round' and 'all the year round' ministry, not only of activity but also of relativity and reality.

Jesus took opportunities as they were presented to Him, and He unfolded whatever He had into those needs around Him. Round peg to round hole. Words of healing into pain. No man spoke like this man.[17] No man showed such wisdom and knowledge when dealing with others. His sufferings made way for His help to be received by sufferers. They abandoned Jonah for the right reasons, while they got rid of Jesus for the wrong ones.

He had more than the Ephesians 4:10-12 gifting within His heart and life. True talents are much wider than these gifts. He was all that men would ever be, as water will rise only to its own level. He was the one who had light and life in abundance. His commitment and expressions of goodness are not presented to us to discourage us, but to encourage us. Every talent we display should sound as a trumpet call into battle. It should be the shout of the one stood at the side as we run the race of life. There is more in the miracles He performed and the words that He spoke than in that alabaster box broken and all its aromatic contents filled the house.[18] Everything He did, unlike Jonah was an expression of love. Talents are love in small parcels. Jesus was the Master, Jonah, as his name suggests, is the dove, carrying the message of the Master.

We are made strong when we look to Jesus

The writer to the Hebrews tell us, urges us with great urgency to look unto Jesus the Author and the Avenue of our faith. If you look at Jonah, as the representative of the old nature, you will only see shipwreck, drowning and complaining. If you look to Jesus your sun will rise again to set no more. In looking to Jesus there is a receiving, there is a resurrecting of all that buried, just as if the flower of seed has heard the call of spring. Talents are tools, they are weapons of a faithful nature, that the Son of God took and destroyed the works of the enemy,[19] and found as signs and wonders, deeds, mercy and peace, revealing the many talents of the Word in John's Gospel. That which is given is more than a miracle, if you never see a miracle, and were to take all the miracles from the life of Jesus, He would still be a man of action, totally consumed in His work of worship through commitment. Jesus was doing something and going somewhere, He was establishing something. Each one of these things He did could fit into the name of God. The acts of Jonah find full expression and commitment in that called rebellion.

Jonah had partial talents with a partial message; yet, even these worked and brought a nation to its knees. When we compare Jonah with Jesus, we see that Jonah is only a skeleton of the Coming One. Jonah had a limited message to a limited people. Most of the prophets had preached to the nation of Israel, but the power of Jesus was to a world locked up in its own ways. Jonah spoke 1,328 words in the book, which bears his name and shame. The city of Nineveh was only about sixty miles in circumference. Yet, God granted him the ability he required for that one mission. He messed it up, but the Greater than Jonah didn't. Many of the words he spoke are forgotten, but not the words of the Saviour. Men hung onto His words, and in the synagogue, the eyes of all in there were fastened on Him as a hinge to a door.[20] Jonah was never nailed to a cross, but the whole book of Jonah is an adequate appeal to live a crucified life. Repentance is a production of resurrection life.

What Jonah had to say touched the captain of the vessel, the crew, it brought a kingdom and a king to its knees. Before the One with every source of help, the whole world will bow, for every knee shall bow and tongue confess Christ to the glory of God the Father.

There was a lack in Jonah's ministry and words

There was no physical healing in the words or works of Jonah, but the life of this complete One abounds with them as flowers on a rockery. There was no washing of feet; there was no withering of a fig tree, only the dying of a gourd, which protected. Jonah fits into the life of Christ as any believer does with his limited application. Jesus was the Way, but Jonah is only a small way, lasting for a few years. It is a way that is filled with holes and stones. Jesus clears it all away that we might understand that Him from heaven was filled with aptitude when answering any and every query. Jonah can only ever be a voice speaking or a finger pointing to the coming One.

When we compare what Jonah was with Jesus it is the comparison of two worlds; it is the comparison of moon with sun and rusty nail with a golden thread. It is Christ who becomes the mirror that we all gaze into, and see our true selves and potential, and as we gaze we grow. Every time we read of Him in the New Testament, He is saying with gentle words, this is the Way, walk you in it. This is the way it should be done. This is the way in which you should let God use you. I am not telling you, I am not holding a conference, seminar or some discussion group, and I am here by example and deed.

Jesus is able to meet every need

The only time His potential was wrapped up was when He was born in a stable and wrapped in swaddling bands. Even on the cross He prayed for their forgiveness and Paradise was uttered by those same lips. His gifts, like His dress was woven throughout from top to bottom without seam. Jesus never said I will perform a partial miracle, or I will give you help, but only meet you half way. He never said I would come again and complete what I was unable to complete. He didn't do it by segments, but He performed a whole work. He did the full and the final thing. Even when He died, he cried 'It is finished!'[21] Jonah did none of these things. Even the book which bears his name seems to illustrate his spirit when it seems to close abruptly.

The Prophet of Old Testament fame came into the city blowing a trumpet or ringing a bell, telling people to repent. Jesus used all His capabilities, particularly in telling the Story of the Prodigal Son, and through other parables (to teach) what repentance really was. He drew life's aspects in picture form, and, then, said 'Go and do like I have said.' Live the story, and never let it become history. Jesus commenced the stream with His tears, and He says to you, flow on, and go on in this stream. Take what God has given and use it until the arm is limp and the hand falls open, until the lips are sealed in death, and the feet walk no more. Then, He will add to what has been given, as interest to an account, when He says "Well done, my good and faithful servant. Enter into the joy of your Lord."

There was a different content in the message of Jesus

The message of Jonah, no matter what his forte was, never contained tears, sweat or blood. There was no cross in it. The only thorns were in his rebellious spirit. There was nothing wrong with Jonah's message; there was just a Pharaoh aspect in it, one whose heart was hard and unyielding.

Even when Jonah prayed out of the belly of the whale it was a prayer which surrounded him. Compare that prayer with the prayer of the Heavenly High Priest in John 17. The span is much larger; the reach is from earth to heaven and back again. All that Jesus was is given to the glorifying of the Father. Every word, as some talent is brought into action, as He touches the heart of God on behalf of the disciples of all ages.

The real object of the dealings of God with him, whose name suggests a dove, was to prepare the heart of the prophet. To release everything he had to offer, and for it to be placed into the hands of God as an altar.

Jesus needed no such preparation, from cradle to cross He delighted to do the will of God. He stands as large as eternity. He comes to us all with every talent we ever desired to have. We ask him for some things, and He tells us that they have been given already. We must take and use what is useful, and that axe head borrowed which has flown from the shaft, needs to be recovered, so that one works with the other, and we begin to build for God, in God and because of God, the source of all genius.

Notes

1	Luke 11:32	9	Luke 24:15	14	John 6:9
2	Mark 14:3	10	Hebrews 10:7,9	15	John 9:4
3	John 2:17	11	Pilgrim's Progress Written	16	Psalm 127:5
4	Hebrews 3:2-8		by John Bunyan, the Bedford	17	John 7:46
5	Colossians 1:19;2:9		Tinker while in prison for	18	Mark 14:3
6	John 14:6		preaching outside the church	19	1 John 3:8
7	Luke 9:51	12	Luke 8:3	20	Luke 4:20
8	Mark 4:39	13	Matthew 27:57,59	21	John 19:30

CHAPTER 3
The burying of your talent

The book of Jonah is the article, which tells the whole story of buried talents. When we read the genealogy of Jonah the son of Amittai, Jonah 1:1 it reads as any other historical record. There are all the ingredients there of spirituality in history, as one chosen of God and ready to serve God. If there were any warts on the face of the prophet, what we read, then, we would be able to accept why he sought to bury his talent by running away from God. At first glance he seems to be whiter than clean. It is when he is placed under the pressures of being used by God that the flaws begin to appear and the ship begins to sink. In the opening verse of the book all seems well. We can all serve God faithfully for a verse or two, even a chapter, but in this matter of using what God has so richly invested in us we have to have no moment that is free from sacredness.

There will always be a ship waiting for the runaway

There will always be a ship waiting for those who want to find their sea legs and use them to run away from that required in using their investment. One mistake might jar the heart but it is the constant mistakes that leave us as something only partial in the world of the dead and the living. That half-hearted is only half a heart.

That done to escape our calling and responsibility will gather around us as a band of renegades ready to hold us fast. The prison that we might find ourselves in behind with one bar and then another. The doors and the walls are added. There is that rising above us until what we have been given cannot be identified. As we look around the prison that disobedience places us in, we have a soul-mate and cell-mate in Jonah. We re-create the story of Jonah within our own lives.

We are those who should soar with eagles

Those who should soar with eagles, scurry with rats and mice, and if you wait the very worm that attacked the gourd will go slithering by. We become proficient Funeral Directors when we are called to be Aeroplane Pilots. We are that which should have been the brothers of stars. There are times when our own compulsions are greater than what God has given to us. We use our own feelings rather than faith, and the net result is abject failure. Like this renegade soldier being neither hot nor cold we can be spewed out of the mouth.[1] When we bury that received we really bury it, placing the benefit as he was in the depths of the deepest sea. We bury it on land or sea. It is impaled on some bad happening. Sometimes it is choked to death through a lack of the fresh breath of the Holy Spirit. All our winds are east winds when we require the north wind of conviction and the south wind of revival. That is sent not for us to lower the anchor but to get back on course. The ministries that came to the luckless one were not sent to nurse him but to heal him. All the happening of the book must not be a walking stick but a jolt to cause us to run freely and straight. How many have turned healing into nursing? What we should do is marked out on the Map of Life by the red blood of the Lord Jesus Christ. Can you see the Sovereign hand at work in this story? Then we must follow the direction it is pointing in. As we get up and go on then we come out of the situation, bringing that dead talent back to life. It was thrown where we think the hand of Destiny can never catch it. The book of Jonah sows hope into a barren field as we read it. That can grow again, it can come to life again. Out of failure can come success. Out of all that seems reckless and lost, God brings triumph. We mustn't live in the chapters of the book of Jonah. Particularly those of doubt and despair, spelling disaster. We must continue to the end and be a winner. Find success in this book, and live in it. Bury your doubts and share your triumphs.

That thrown on one side and buried can be used

That thrown on one side as the jawbone of an ass, which Samson used, was later used to refresh a dying man.[2] How many had walked by that buried talent and never seen its potential? Buried in a former history and on a wasteland it required a hand to rescue it. The book and life of this prophet is like that. Drink and taste here, then go away and be the very best God has called you to be. You might not be the greatest thing or the most dedicated thing but do not be the dead and buried thing! Come from it refreshed and ready to serve. Skip where you have stumbled, and walk where you have been sitting and waiting. You may do a million things, but if not one of those things is what God requires of you, the other things will never produce deep happiness and a sense of well being. In the million activities it is the one marked out by the sacred hand needing to be accomplished. When we respond as this battered man did, it brings us from burying to living. See Jonah climb out of a bad location, and go on to be successful.

Jonah was the son of Amattai, Jonah 1:1 meaning 'truth telling'. It is all told as it is. It is God who does the speaking and telling. There are times when we never hear from this seaman. We think he has gone to sleep and he has. There is that about him long dead and submerged. Long before the ship was ready for breaking and sinking he was buried. We don't just bury; we bury in a hopeless mess. The first spade of earth, the first opening up of the hole to bury his enabling was when he went in the opposite direction to that which the Almighty had beckoned.

This book is a true Gospel Herald telling and training for future trials, 'to do or not to do, to be or not to be' that is the question which is answered. It is a manual, telling, teaching and revealing what we should do to be a victor. The contents of the heart are turned out, and God, through the wind of the Holy Spirit blows all the chaff away, planting the good seed in the heart of the reader and hearer. We are called to be witnesses to a hurting heart sometimes. The truth stands in this witness box, and gives its own story and verdict. There is that Hand reaching out and pulling us back to God. That same hand is part of God, seeking to unearth that long forgotten and buried in the very depths of our memories. What you have turned into an old bone, is taken and turned into a useful weapon of warfare. The Caleb of Scripture whose name means 'a dog' will come and dig it up, and then the Master of the dog will clothe it to make it into a man as He made Eve, the Mother of all living out of a bone in the dust.

God raises his warriors from different backgrounds

Tradition says he was the grandson of the woman of Zarephath in Zidon, raised from the dead by Elijah in 1 Kings 17:24. Jonah is also mentioned in 2 Kings 14:25. He lived and worked during the reign Jeroboam the 2nd, who reigned in Jerusalem for forty-one years. He was from the tribe of Zebulun, the tribe of dwelling, the tribe who kept an open door to other nations, which Jonah wanted to close, and that is why he wanted to push his ability out of sight. With an all-seeing, knowing

God, that is a difficult task. He was a prophet and a teacher in Israel. He came from Gatherer, Gath-hepher, 2 Kings 14:25 'the place of the well'.[3] In the hiding what should have been used, he turned the well into a hell. It was really Gath, where Goliath and his brothers came from that David and his men had to destroy.[4] From the same place as large destructive giants come those who would rebel against the known will of God. Goliath is alive and operates in our rebellion. In fact, as we shall read later, he was sent in one direction, and he went in the total opposite direction. He was told to go to Nineveh meaning 'fishing'. He went to Tarshish which means 'breaking'. You receive the intervention that you give yourself to. If you go to the place of breaking, you will be broken. Buried deep in the sea, when he was thrown over the side of the ship, all is dark around him. He did arrive at Joppa suggesting 'beauty'. There was that which could and would grow again. There is that latent within all waiting for the kiss of life. There are such beauties in you waiting to leap into a resurrection.

Jonah is one of the more honest prophets of God. He does not try to hide the fact that he sought to disobey God, and, in doing so buried his future, by letting it sail away on a ship and being thrown into the sea and being swallowed by a whale. This 'dove' (which is the meaning of Jonah) wrote his own history with the beak of a bird and was so open, as open as a book. He wrote it for us to read, placing as some advert on manuscript for all those who would limit their capabilities to read, learn and then run for Refuge. What he writes is written on the face of the page for all to read. It is written on the wall that we call the world for all to read. He did with his pen what they do in China, when they have news they post it on the wall for the entire city to come and see to read. In the social history of England, if you owed money to a local shop and the debt was not paid they placed your name on a list in the shop window for every passer by to see and read. This book of Jonah is just like that. Such a great life being placed on some list and staying there! The talent is buried indeed!

We can lose the direction of our destiny

When we lose our sense of calling and direction, the front becomes the back, and the back becomes the front. If you were to write your own history, what different colours you might etch into the picture! Drawing a curtain to hide a worn chair, placing a table over a worn patch in the carpet. Yet, he places in everything good and bad. There is no economy with the truth. The Pandora's box has the lid lifted from it. We see anger as great as any swelling sea. The moods are there as unreliable as the waves of the sea. There is envy and jealousy as large as any whale. The frustrations are seen as seaweed winding itself around his hands and feet. The feeling of hopelessness, like one trying to empty the sea with a spoon is not only seen but also it is heard. It can read as the diary of the modern man. He never seeks to vindicate himself. He never says others were wrong and I was right. The book leaves us with a strong presence of God and the willingness to take the blade of the Spirit and unearth whatever part of us has been interred and for whatever reason.

We are as foolish as the Foolish Virgins in the New Testament, and when we turn from our goals we need to turn to the book of Jonah, and as you read it, as you turn the page, your gift can be turned up and placed back where it should be.[5] God always leaves his bookmark in the shape of a cross where we should turn to. We find it where we lost it. We take it where we let it go. We lift it up for all to see, taking it from its hiding place, which, usually is the heart. It is in some happening that affected the heart that we encase that tool.

We can all learn from Jonah

The book of Jonah has been called 'A Masterpiece of Literature'. It has been hung in the gallery of time for all to gaze at. It is a ready companion to the book of Ruth, Esther, the parables of the Good Samaritan and the Prodigal Son. It is a missionary story with the prayer of the missionary in chapter 2. It is a prison epistle, written out of an experience in the stomach of a whale, with weeds as prison bars, and lungs as doors. From that pit of pity we hear an echo into our own hearts. As we meditate, we stand on the side looking in. We look over the edge into the abyss.

There is such a thing as the school of Jonah. Whales might be found in a 'school', but here is better learning, and higher degrees. We enter that school and schooling when we acknowledge what we have done in burying that which would bring life. We bury the very resurrection power bringing hope to all when we deny that which is God crafted.

The providence of God is the best ship

Without a promise, Jonah throws himself onto the providence of Lordship. That is the best and only 'ship' to sail on! There is a plan, God's plan, and God made it work. He moved heaven, earth and sea to bring it into its fullness. This man was only a small pawn, but he was, as far as God was concerned, the most important part of the designed plan. The repentance of Nineveh was required. The Mighty One's greater intention was the training of the heart. All things were for its future development and accomplishment.

There is no record of time in this book of Jonah's jottings. It is as if time doesn't matter. It doesn't, for in the dealings of Father Time, time stands still. Eternity is now with us, a true Emmanuel. What happened to the servant of the Lord can happen, and does happen in all ages and stages of Christian life and growth.

We see the life of the prophet from every angle

It treats what happens to us from the other angle, almost as if the hammer or the trowel that you build with is writing the story. What a story it is! It is one of laughter, tears and great joy. It is a book of adventure, of sailing and sinking. It gives us such descriptive language, Jonah 1:11, 13, the old King James rendering "The sea 'wrought'", as if it worked and walked on its own accord, carrying everything with it. Going for a walk like a strong man, carrying the prophet with buried potential with him under its arm. The sea carried him as some shepherd carrying the sheep, but a more cruel suggestion is here. He is born along like that caught as a victim in the mouth of that destroying jaw of the wolf, bear or lion. The sea is there to carry him off.

This book has nothing in common with other books of the prophets. The only connection is that a prophet writes it. The prophecies found in the book are not uttered but they are revealed. Each prophecy is acted out in a deed and word. The writer does not look backward as Moses did when he wrote. He does not look forward as Isaiah or Daniel. He looks inward at his own heart. It is like the epistle of Paul to Philemon, the epistle of the heart, the epistle giving a new start.

If we turn away from one thing, a city like Nineveh, there will be a greater thing to come to us like the raging sea or a whale that will just eat us up. Cast on some island, as a drifter is the end product. What use are talents on a desert island? If there are no building materials. We shall be lost to be found as we throw ourselves on the mercy of God, for that was the only seat in the belly of the whale where Jonah could sit. From a slimy altar he called unto the 'Restorer of the Breaches' to restore him.

God prepares his servants

In this writing, there are six things prepared by God. A wind is prepared twice, the fish, the sea, the gourd and worm. To make the perfect number of seven there is another thing being prepared and that is the prophet Jonah. When God prepares anything, that is only the beginning of the matter. The vessel has to be filled with treasure. It has to become a treasure trove in itself. All, six things prepared, are schoolteachers to bring him to God. There were so many knocks at his heart's door, planned and presented by God. Did you ever read any part of Holy Writ where the Lord Jehovah was engaged in such activity! All these things prepared simply to prepare the heart of the servant. God can triumph easily with those branches of nature, but when dealing with the human heart, ah, that is quite another thing! That sea was some sea in size and volume, but not as raging as the human heart and the disposition of a man. It is easier for Neptune to control whales than the will of a man. This is why we bury our inherent qualities, making us different from rat or rabbit, horse or kangaroo, our God-given abilities to create and make.

The nature of the messenger is in all of us

Nineveh as a city has long vanished into the mist of yesterday's vapour from the stream which flowed by. Jonah remains, for he lives in the one reading this book. If you are ever thumbing a lift to get out of the will of God, there are fleets of cars waiting to take you. The docks are full of ships as the airport has many waiting planes. There are so many happenings presented as holes in which to bury your genius in. Coffins do not cover themselves, there are plenty of others waiting to do it. The coffin or the flowers are not death itself they are just tokens of what has happened. These tokens are in this book of Jonah for us to see as signs warning of the charging bull.

No other bible book mixes together strength and weakness, grace and hope, burial and resurrection like this one does. All is figured here to help you. The end of the matter is the matter of the end. God triumphs and all you possess is fully used to deliver with. You will discover through life becoming your teacher and in the many mistakes, that God is bigger than you. He is your God, and from Him comes every perfect gift. He is above and below all. God's hand is on the rudderless whale. The Captain of skies and seas has the winds in His hands. Worms are not above being used by this great Person.

John Calvin remarks 'When we have been faithful with our own nation and people, then God has new frontiers reserved for us. There are other cities and peoples, but first of all we must be proven at home.' L. Paula, a modern day Evangelist, writing about modern Evangelists said 'Before I invited one, I would like to know what their home life and church life was like.' The book of Jonah grants us these insights in the making or the marring of a man or a prophet. Through the book we take a God's eye view of the inner life of the man with the talent for preaching and travelling.

Notes

1	Revelation 3:16	4	1 Samuel 17:4. 2 Samuel 21:22
2	Judges 15:15-19	5	Matthew 25:1-11
3	2 Kings 14:25		

CHAPTER 4

The challenge to use your talent

Jonah 1:1, 'The word of the Lord came unto Jonah'. It had to get into Jonah, until he was brought to that place of full surrender and commitment to the area of expedition God was pointing him to. This word will make you what the word is. The voice of God will come and challenge you until God is operating in all His fullness of design. Each tool and each weapon is used in its own realm. It brings the most success when being used for what it was created for and what God had placed within this one had to go to where it could be greatly used. We all operate the best in that area that we have been called to. If you are only called to be a pea in a whistle then that is the best place you could be. There might be a calling to train and work as a computer expert. If that is true then be true! The challenge is to bring all of us into that where we will operate usefully and successfully. It is operating in what you were created for.

Without being challenged we are just as this man

Without the challenge of the Word of God, Jonah is just another man without much purpose. Just a rat in the 'rat race of life.' Just a sea-going pirate or a rat ready to swim from the vessel when it is about to sink. It is the Word that takes the talents we have, and seeks to challenge us to use them. You can place everything from the intellect to your faithfulness, and everything else of talent form on this word. This message from God exposes and expounds that required by God. That given and received is for a purpose, and we become mature in its operation. The talent can make the man what he should be. Until we are challenged, one thought, one deed is as good as the other. We all have to work for a living, but few are living in their work. The two ships in the harbour or dry dock are just the same. It is when they sail forth that the real discovery comes into its own. The sword of Goliath is just as another sword until it is taken and used in a battle.[3] It is so easy to have a shop window or a shopping list talent, where it doesn't mean a thing, and we are never challenged, never told what to do or receive any instruction. It was when this chosen one was told to go and to do, the flaws appeared. It was when the word of

God was specific, as to what God expected that he was weighed in the balances and found wanting.[1]

He was only told to go to one place

He wasn't told to go to a thousand places, and, therefore went to none. He was told to go fully armed to one place, the place of fishing, meaning Nineveh.[2] The water might be wine, but it is in the tasting of it, in it passing through lips and teeth and sliding over the taste buds that the real truth dawns as to the vintage and flavour. When it strikes the back of the palate we know the difference between wine and water. We can be ever so obedient to the Lord when we are never told what to do. That left to roam without direction and command will become a runaway reject. We can be all ears, and never listen, all mouth that never speaks, all eyes and never see.

Where and when this direction came we know not. Was he sitting, sleeping, eating in his own home or just watching sailing ships? The conviction from God knew where to find him, and where to send him.

When God chooses to use that which has been granted us, the calling is the enabling. If He sends you along a rock-strewn path He will provide strong shoes. Those shoes are the best for the blessing as we are going. For each stormy sea He has a good vessel to provide so that you have a safe passage. It is never just a challenge for challenge's sake. It is something from God to put us into action. He doesn't force us; He just makes us willing to go. It is that sent, even as God arranges your circumstances so that you hear and you obey. The New Testament word for 'believe' has in it the suggestion of hearing and obeying. To listen enough to obey, to treat what is uttered as final. He had to become the echo of that word, even as the note will correspond to the trumpet and the note played through it. It was a Sovereign Word, a sure word, settled word. Settled in heaven to make an impact on earth. He could trust any and every gift to it. Over three hundred times in the Old Testament scriptures we have the golden glorious phrase 'The word of the Lord came.' It came so that he might go. It told what he might say. It directed so that he wouldn't be lost. It sounds louder than any other word we listen to without shouting. It comes and it resides where it finds His throne. There it sits to rule until the life becomes as some well adorned and ordered palace.

That given to direct us must be obeyed

When we are challenged it must not be treated as snow falling or water running through a brook, but more like sun shining. It is not that lasting for a day. This was no sudden shout or burst of laughter. It wasn't meant to be, as a joke told, to be forgotten by the time required think your next thought. It was to be with this servant all the days of his life. As the fire of the tabernacle it must never go out.[4]

That echo of a whisper from God, which Elijah heard in the still, small voice could come to you from many sources, as some fountain springing forth in many directions.[5] This was a telling, directing, disciplining word from God. In it was the heart of God for the people of Nineveh. It was as if God was tuning the instruments, and gathering them all together in orchestrated fashion. This word was to be as profoundly moving as any great piece of music, digging as deep as the talent was buried. There was that to be sent out to that Great City, and the man whose name means a 'dove' had the gifting to do it. God was about to stir that, which had settled, and He does, almost fluttering like the eagle over the nest. The dove had gone to its own window to watch the world go by.

That received will remove all restrictions

That word removes every restriction, and it grants boldness. The saying is fulfilled as we respond 'A man's gift makes room for him'.[6] It opens doors and throws down barriers, for it brings him before great men. Smith Wigglesworth, one of the Pentecostal pioneers in the United Kingdom used to say 'God has said it, I believe it, that settles it.' That sort of response sharpens the blade turning the two edged blade towards the enemy. The opposite was the truth for this messenger. What was meant to further him, hindered him, because he let his emotional instability, narrow, religious bigotry and what he thought, get in the way. It was as if some masterpiece had been painted, and then, a little child came and threw paint over it, thereby destroying the whole, and making it worthless. The Eternal wants to take us from finger painting of Kindergarten to real artistry. Wait a moment, and see what God is able to do when he adds the red blood of Jesus to it. He does what the famous artist did when presented with a handkerchief with a blot on it. He drew around it, and made the blot the head of the flower. Out of the mistakes God makes men. Men without mistakes, men even with their mistakes.

That given by God is only lent to us

When God has given, God will take the gift and the one who possesses it. They are only lent to the prophet, but he seeks to treat them as his own. There are rather large departments in the heart where we place things we think belong to us. Over the door the word 'stolen' is written. The lock to each door is within. We have locked the key within our own hearts. Each gift, with an account of how it was used must be given back to the Giver with usury. As God takes hold of the one, He takes hold of the other. Many a person has failed, and through that failure others have been given the opportunity to go. As it is broken it finds its healing in the word of God. The only way to realise that given is by a breaking and making. There is one redeeming feature in this story. We can't see a second Jonah waiting to be used by God. There is no second whale, but there is a second chance. Men reject that marked by the word 'second' they think it means inferior but it never does with Deity. The Designer only had one man, and this was the man. He had no other plans, all was committed to this project. God had made no provision for failure. He expects you to succeed, and nothing succeeds like success. Where God has planted, watered and sown, He expects a harvest. He expects us to know to go when He says so.

That talent of Jonah would give all the people of Nineveh an opportunity to repent. It would introduce life. It would have established Lordship in that area. One thing worked alongside another. As you surrender, who can tell whom you will help and encourage. As a word received it is put to the enemy then it will not only trip up but slash and kill removing all impediments to response and responsibility. God's pleading is his placing for racing. Knowing, listening and hearing is translated into going.

If you take care to do what God asks of you, then God will take care of the city, the family, the future and all of your failings. That response, the correct response, would make so many others so happy, from the king on the throne to the beasts in the field. Even the sun will shine for you as you obey. That around, instead of it being out of place, will find its place. Here is where broken loaves and fishes are turned into dishes.

Each one has so many different talents

Jonah's talents were many, even as many as the feathers on the dove he represents. Most commentators emphasise his preaching. There are a host of angels involved in his life. Like you, he has talents, which he has never thought of. They are there, but because we can't describe or name them, even number them, we reject them. Commencing when his call came, the challenge to go and preach, trace with the finger of the crucified Christ how many things come into operation in his life. All are called what they are by God. It is not what men call them; it is how we use them, and our availability to God. When the question comes from God, you be the answer. You are the door to the outside world, and let God open you so fully and freely, that you are taken off your hinges.

'Preach the preaching that I bid you.' Do the doings of God. Live the life. Express His love freely as the cherry hanging on the branch. Make that count which I have made you. Give away that which I have given you. As you use your ability, God gives you another, until it is pressed down, shaken together and running over. It is the shaking together which results in the running over. For those who have concrete convictions that are the wrong ones, shape and size, all mixed up and set like concrete God wants to re-design. In that mixture He wants to replace the pebbles with pearls.

Talents are what we are best at. Sometimes, they are what we will let the Talent Giver make us the best at. Talent can be turned into genius through obedience and hard work. They are the things that make you different from others. A vacuum cleaner is a vacuum cleaner, a table is a table, a chair is a chair, but what are you? You were called into the kingdom for such a time as this. If you think you have no talents to be challenged, then, learn to smile well and speak well of, and for, your King. Give away a sandwich with a warm hand. Feed your enemy and heap coals of fire on his head to melt him or her down.

We forget that enabling belongs to Jehovah

R. C. Trench, writing on the word 'talent' states 'Men tend to forget the end for which their talents were given them; they may count them as something they have gotten; they may turn them to selfish ends, they may deny they were given them at all.' Your special gift, your special aptitude must be given an account of. Each will be called to answer for his own. Talents will tell their own tale, as you stand by.

A proper response would have saved him from getting wet and seasick. There would have been much more than just seaweed for breakfast, dinner and tea, while eating at the place called 'whale'. His bedroom would have had a different décor. It would have rescued him from a turbulent sea and cutting waves. The flood of your own tears and the constant remorse could be wiped away. The Word, whatever source it comes from, returns to the sender, and takes us back to God. In that Word is a hand and a harp. It is a challenge to use what you have. I wonder how many years he had been in training for this moment, which led to him being shattered as one of the pieces of wood in the ship's deck. He concluded this portion of his life as a harp unstrung and a song unsung. God will always send you deeper into his perfect will. No, He will call you into it for it is Himself that we seek to serve, and not just His will. Wherever He calls us to and wherever He sends us, He is there. He is calling us to be with Himself. Jesus ordained the disciples that 'they might be with Him.'[7] It is not just talents, but it is a heart surrendered, and that in it can be a gift from God.

Notes

1   Jonah 1:1,2
2   Jonah 1:2
3   1 Samuel 22:10
4   Leviticus 6:9,13
5   1 Kings 19:12
6   Proverb 18:16
7   Mark 3:14

CHAPTER 5

The refusal to use your talent

God had told the prophet what to do, and which direction to travel in. He should have gone to Nineveh, as a fully armed messenger with all his talents. The word 'talent' can describe the Red Indian with his arrows on fire going into the attack. He went to Joppa, to catch a boat to Tarshish.[1] There is a complete reversal of things once he understands what God means. When we refuse to do God's will, it makes us unusable and less than God intended us to be. Then we travel as some flying trapeze artist whose rope has broken under the weight of the snatch and grab. What might, with perfect balance be taking us so high, brings us so low that we can see worms from the underneath. That given is hidden as we close our hand upon it to seclude it from the passing shadow of God. To neglect your impetus, do not to throw it away, but just refuse to use it. Let it become as wax running down the side of the candle.

You must be what God wants you to be

It is a matter of being what He wants you to be before you can go where He wants you to go. The important thing is what we are 'before God' before it is declared what we are 'before men' men are guessing when they are giving glory. God is all-knowing and showing us exactly what we are. Men are saying what they see Jehovah is telling what he knows. You can cover up from one but 'all things are open and naked before Him with whom we have to do.' This scripture is a picture of torture taken from the Romans. They placed a dagger under the chin of a victim, and the prisoner was forced to look up into the face of his captor or let his head fall onto the blade.[2] Character is greater than talent. Character is greater than charter. The Master is greater than lesson taught or lesson received. It is character, which holds competence together, just as the map has in it all the areas of the world. Jonah might have had the best gift since creation, but without a wholesome character he would always be as the fruit in the pip.

There are certain avenues presented to the preacher by God, and his abilities should have flown along those avenues. Not to heed the call results in a fall. We never fall forward, it is always backwards and downwards, so low that we finish in the whale of our own making. Surely going to the city, seeing all the beautiful sights and architecture was better than sitting looking at the blank wall of the lining of a fish's stomach. What Jonah was to the whale, the will of God was to the prophet, it couldn't be digested. All this leads to is to a backward fall into the past, and as we fall and faint we crush the very future promised by God under the weight of our refusal. What a way, ultimately to hold him down! Using this great monster of a fish as a weight. Boxed up in that sea thing, so that he couldn't escape.

The challenge of the Word is often repeated

Four times in the book of the prophet we have the phrase 'saying'.[3] The word of God came saying. Each word spoken is meant to help us in our refusal. God is always saying 'I have not refused you.' He stretches out His hand all day long to His people. When the hand was nailed to the cross it was that the moulding, raising and helping hand might be stretched out forever. All can come and use it as a covert in the time of storm. It is the word coming from the heart of God, and leads us into that part of His heart we call will. It is the only word. The danger is that we listen to the noise of the sea, the waves and the captain of the ship rather than God. There are so many voices shouting to us and at us and not one of them is without significance.[4] 'Signification' means 'without sound or sense.' The voice of God is not the uncertain sound of a trumpet calling into battle. That word is a light over the face of the sea, it is a rope over the boat to help us out of the watery grave, even before we enter it. Sometimes, it is not what God delivers us from, but what He seeks to keep us from. 'Deliver us from evil', should read 'deliver us from the Evil One.' In the refusal Goliath defeats David, the day is turned into night, black night holding all the fright and fear you can imagine around the next corner. What might have been a small stream, suddenly grows into a deep sea and a restless storm, which carries all before it. There is a certain restlessness about withholding, the stability goes, and the emotions begin to roll like the waves of a sea.

There is that descending into declension

The moment he refuses to obey that which is obedience to God, another word creeps into the King James narrative of what happened.

The word 'down' appears four times. It isn't the anchor to stabilise us with. It is the descending of the rock thrown into the sea. This is another word, different from the word, which God brought to him. This is the word of the saint turned sinner. It is the word of the person who will not use what has been given. This word 'down' is found in Jonah 1:3,3,5. & 2:6. we descend to the very depth where we have buried that optimism granted by God. We share the nature of the cruel sea in the refusal. The word 'down' used figuratively means to fall. When we say 'no', that 'no' is one of the steps we descend into the bottom of things rather than going to the top. It is the bottom rung of the vocabulary ladder. Here Jonah came to a standstill. There was no further progress until God was allowed to take and use what had been given. Even the fish might swim, the tide can come in and out, and plankton moves freely, but not the son of Gath, where he came from. Being from that city there is something of a Goliath within him that requires defeating. Human nature defies God daily. Putting on one side one thing, he takes to himself something far greater and more demanding than God ever expected. A corrupted call will lead to a rotten core.

The mission field he should have gone to

He should have gone to Nineveh, the place of fishing. This was part of the gift of God. As the disciples, if we have rod, boat or net, then we must fish. There comes seasons and moments when we must re-cast both net and rod. It was a great and mighty city, the equivalent of London or Birmingham in England, in his day, comparing size with size, and populations as they would be at that time. The walls of the city were so thick; you could drive a chariot along them. Do not get the idea that he refused because it was so small and beneath him or so large that it was above him. When God is in charge, then everything is levelled to your level. God presents that which you can do. His callings are still His enabling. When God says go, He gives you the first two letters of His name 'Go'. The very spirit of the man was so small; it couldn't include other people. The Eternal's 'goes' are not His groans or growls but they are the gold of His will and ways.

The city was built by Nimrod who has this testimony that he began to be a 'Mighty hunter before the Lord'. The American spy plane system called AWAX has one aeroplane called 'Nimrod'. Genesis 10:11 tells us it stood on the eastern bank of the Tigress. It was there as a monument to a man. God wanted Jonah to go there, and in the hearts of the people build a monument to God. God builds better and bigger than men do when he can build on our surrender, and through what we give as our forté. There is something larger than walls, more open than gates and stronger than stones that God requires to build. Not in time, but through truth.

The city is mentioned eight times in this little book with a big God and a small prophet.

Elohim wants to make the man as large as Nineveh, as large as the sea and as large as the fish. In the book of Matthew in the New Testament it stands as a picture of judgement. In Nahum 2:8, it is described as a pool of water. No doubt, there were fish swimming here. What was a small pool filled with sweet water was turned into a raging sea by the salt of rebellion. The All Wise never sends you with your potential to fish where there are no fish. The Master's paths never lead us to a plunge. There is nothing ending in a dead-end about them. They all have openings at each turn, which lead into something larger. 'My sheep shall go in and out and find pasture', Jesus said.[5]

When your nature becomes a restrictive practice

The fly in this ointment was the fact that he didn't agree with what God wanted. Where was he when Elohim laid the foundations of the earth? He sits on the circle of the earth joining both ends together and keeps it as a circle, so that it can't be made into a square by some scientist.[6] The Jewish nature was apt to forget the God who forgives, or the God of pardons, as He is called.[7] Maybe he didn't want to present a God who changes his mind. Jehovah doesn't, only in the sense of playing music when you change key. Jonah might get laughed at. The 'laughing stock' was not considered to be one of his many degrees. Thinking of the history of God's people, he would know that the walls of that great city Jericho fell flat. Why didn't El Shaddai intend to do the same, here? He forgot, and we forget that Sovereignty, sometimes, conquers all and takes prisoners with a gentle word binding them. He doesn't trip them up or kill them, He, sometimes pours healing virtue into their wounds, and as those wounds heal, they surrender all their powers to Him.

When Jesus said, "I will make you to become fishers of men."[8] The word 'fishes' is from a root word meaning 'salt'. Their talent was to be of a cutting, tangy nature. This man could have stayed the corruption sooner, rather than later. How many perished while he was going around in the circle of the sea?

We respond far quicker in rebellion than in obedience

He went quicker to Tarshish than he would ever have gone to Nineveh. He repented, and then he moved as a bird with six wings, or as something jet propelled. It is quite amazing, when we want to put down what God has commanded that we should take up, how quickly we accomplish it. The stone going from the sling as David conquers Goliath bears no comparison with the speed that he travelled at when he obeyed. To use a modern phrase he put his skates on, serving with alacrity. God played the tune and he danced to it readily with great freedom.

We all arrive at breaking point instead of boiling point

Tarshish is the place of breaking. When we refuse to bend in the hands of God, we break under the strain of the rod of rebellion. Just as Elijah had to come to Zarephath, 1 Kings 17:9, the place of melting and smelting[9], to be melted, to be smelted, as the furnace is heated. It is the place where silver,ore and gold are taken from the rock. Jeremiah 10:9, we discover that silver, iron, metal and tin were beaten into plate shape. God desires to do this for us all. There will be many places like this called Tarshish before we fully recover and are clothed in our right minds, being all used up for the Master. He could leave this place as the knight in shining armour. In the whole armour of Royalty rather than being clad in Adam's coat. Of his own choosing in refusing to let go and let God, he came here. The moment we withhold that which doesn't belong to us, the winds start to blow; the sea passage gets rough. The whale begins to grow from a small herring. All these things are against me. In refusal; all hell is set free to operate as it pleases, and with all its evils of human nature are set free. 'Force me to render up my sword, and I shall conqueror be.' We fall where we started, before we ever commenced. There is that which would tie us to the starting blocks.

The heart and not the head requires enlargement

The heart and not the head of Jonah requires enlarging, so that in his heart, there is a table with food on it, a chair with a cushion, and light which has been lit, made for these people of Nineveh. Dr Strong gives the meaning of Tarshish as 'breaking, preparing, disciplining'. Dr Robert Young says it means 'that which is hard'.

Unknowingly, he enters the school of God. God goes before him to prepare many a lesson. Gesenius in his Hebrew Dictionary declares the meaning as 'subjection'.[10] It is astounding what we subject ourselves to when we do not use our faculties. The Eternal allows us to go to that which suggests a cross. There the moulding and restoring takes place. That which has gone from the mind, that fallen from the hand is taken up and used again. It is taken from the cloth of our own covering, to be uncovered by God.

Many times it is back to Tarshish, back to the drawing board. God draws many wonderful pictures here, and He gives us many lessons of love. Backwards to take us forwards and onwards in the work of God. Suddenly, the span of God's hand becomes larger as Jonah is dealt with. 1 Kings 22:48; tells us, warning us the ships of Tarshish were broken. It is where God breaks the ships, when we become pirates and the masters of our own destiny. From our breaking God does the making. He brings us through into an obedient nature. Ships can sail because they have captains and crew to govern them. Man is much more complex as we see in this moving picture before us. There has to be a place of crucifying the flesh. God lets us go there to be changed. To make you into the whole person He wants you to be. If there is that partial understanding of all that Jehovah Nissi is, you judge Him as you judge a book by its cover, and we only know half, then God will take us back to school, and, it is sometimes called by the name of this place. The 'school of fish' had another student, but he was made more like the one that got away.

When broken we grow in grace

The name Tarshish was taken into maritime language and used metaphorically of great ships, carrying great burdens. There was a dock here. There was a quayside, and there always is where God will help us to unload the overload. It is where anchors can be dropped until we rest in the bosom of Abraham, meaning the Bay of Abraham.[11] Until we float with assurance holding us in God. Until there is a certain lift in our spirits, and we take up that which we have been taken up for.

There is a false beauty to be avoided

He went to Joppa, the place of false beauty, and the place of false assurance. The beast can be turned into a beauty. It is the residence where things can be manufactured, rather than being of miracle quality. Jezebel that wicked woman holds seminars here on skin beauty. The area of covering up that we have covered up our usefulness, and we are as a gold ingot hidden in silk cloth. It is the place of pretence. That which isn't really real, where we all love to play hide and seek with God. The training of the hypocrite takes place here. The cost of each lesson is high; you pay for them with sincerity and truth. You know how we used to put our face to the wall and count to a hundred, while others were hiding. We do this, and for the numbers counted we have scriptural verses which we use as we read the word of God. We think that it is all right, but we are still hiding as we are counting. When we open our eyes, as a child, we think the big, bad troublesome thing will not be there. We find it is the Land of the Giant where everything is turned into a pillar of salt.

He went down to Joppa to have a false beauty applied to him. The toad can inflate itself until it looks larger than it is. Some creatures do it to frighten others. We think the larger the shadow the less there will be of the sun on another's pathway and walk before God. Love is not boastful or proud. If I am not blessed I will make sure they are not encouraged. In being used by the One above, we require an adornment of our own. We are accepted in the Beloved, but we must all receive of His grace, grace upon grace. From this modern seaport of Jaffa, he took a ship. This was no Jaffa orange, more like a lemon because of his refusal to travel by God's compass. I am sure, he took the first ship, and the first opportunity was greedily accepted as one with a strong appetite.

To hear him pray, you would have thought he had wholly followed the Lord. When he could have said 'Nothing in my hand I bring', it sounded spiritual, but it was empty because of the dedication laid on one side. That had fallen from him as some soldier lets all go when sorely wounded. There was all that here which could be found in a paintbrush.

It is beauty, which is no beauty at all. It is beauty for ashes. There is the easing of the conscience, which we think, is beauty, but it is deformed as crushed clay and twisted straw. We must all come to Gilgal, 'the cutting of the flesh' and the destruction of natural beauty, and what we have designed. There is a beauty, a secret beauty in that withheld. It is in the feeling of satisfaction and desire. The deep beauty of the heart comes as we enter the Secret Place of the Most High to behold the beauty and glory of His presence. Seeing His garments there in prayer we bring one out with us to clothe us in new nature.

The real beauty of the new nature

The most beautiful thing in the world is a talented person. It is better than a masterpiece. It is not pencilled in but drawn from within. That person who has the beauty of Zion is like the sky with its sun, moon, stars and clouds. All your beauty is plastic unless it is brought to you and produced in you as you exercise your nobility. The soldier who fought well was referred to as talented. He had the wounds and the bloodstains to prove it. The shepherd, who kept his sheep from wolves, never leaving them to a hireling was spoken of as being gifted. The captain of the vessel, who came through the storm and at great cost brought it into port, was designated talented.

Notes

1 Jonah 1:3
2 Hebrews 4:13
3 Jonah 1:1; 3:1,7; 4:2,4
4 1 Corinthians 14:10
5 John 10:9
6 Isaiah 40:22
7 Micah 7:18
8 Mark 1:17
9 1 Kings 17:9
10 Genesius Hebrew
   Chaldee Lexicon
   published by Baker
   Book House
11 Luke 16:23

CHAPTER 6
The cost of hiding your talent

There are so many spheres we would touch, so many beautiful things to enter into when we do not hide that which God has surrounded us with. Talents are the weapons of our warfare.[1] If we use what has been placed at our disposal we win. If we turn away from the gifts and callings of God that become our challenges and the purpose of our existence we become world losers. Others win the prizes and take the trophies We take the sand and rake the leftovers. Instead of the largeness of His hand, we only feel the strength of His finger. Instead of being in that Pacific Ocean, which suggests peace, we find ourselves in some pond in the back garden, playing with rubber ducks and plastic ships.

We bury the talent when we become possessive

As children we played village cricket. It used to be so enjoyable. The problem was when one young man provided the bat, ball and stumps; we even played on his father's strip of land. If anything offended him, or he was told what to do, bold out when he thought he shouldn't be, even if he hadn't made the runs he expected, he took bat, ball, stumps and land from us. To some if it isn't theirs by inheritance or obtained by strength, they will not share it with the weak. 'There is that which scatters and yet tends to increase.'[2] That withheld makes us so small. Here is the spirit of Jonah we are dealing with. As that young man with his cricketing weapons, he could never play another game until he returned with his gifts.

There is a cost involved when we bury the talent

The man who heard from God had to pay his own fare when travelling on the ship. It is quite acceptable when travelling at our own expenses and going to our own place we have a bottomless pocket. It seems sometimes as if that is being shoved in through the hole the money is falling out of. We pay with more than money. We pay with that related to the majesty of God. There will always be the gold of glory surrendered into the quick silver of seeing it happen here and now. There is always a cost involved when we lay down our essentials for God. If you go to your own destination, you pay your own fare. In the long-term contract, you pay for your folly. We don't pay in the coinage of the king, but we pay for it in lost opportunities, and the possibilities of doing more for God. There are sharp pieces of wood coming from the cross. The thorn from His crown comes to goad us. The nails from the cross of Christ, as with the thorns, turn inwards. It is hard for us to kick against the goads. I am sure, that each wave of the sea, which went over the head of this one under consideration, shouted loudly in his ears as a challenge to change from God.

The great cost of burying the talent

The largest expense we incur in life is when we lose spiritual values. The sheep may lose its wool, the tree might lose its leaves, but there is a far greater loss with the man of God's choosing. We become as the fisherman without a rod, and a soldier without weapons. It costs far more to bury something than bless with it. When he travelled in the boat it was third class travel at first class price. Once we have surrendered one thing, anything else soon follows. When we let go of one thing, it is easier to give up the more valuable things. We hardly notice if our shoe loses one stitch in the leather, but that one makes the way for the whole to fall apart, and to cease to be a shoe. 'A stitch in time saves nine.' It is the little principles denied that make for a great calamity. The word 'scruples' that we all need when using that given to us for a cause and a challenge, means 'sand gathered between the toes.' it chaffs, it hurts, it causes pain to work for God.

In denying God what He has given we become the empty jewel box, just for ornamentation, but not having any real content. Thereby fulfilling the proverb 'empty cans make most rattle.' I have discovered the name of the ship he travelled on wasn't called 'Discovery', 'Mayflower', or 'Endeavour.' The name it had was 'From Riches to Rags.' We all sail at some time on the 'Titanic.' All that are impoverished by a peevish spirit travel with him on it. They become members of the crew. 1 Corinthians 9:27, the apostle Paul doesn't want to be a 'castaway'. He doesn't want to be rejected as part of the cargo on the vessel which is jettisoned. When the sea gets rough, they toss all unwanted things overboard, and the paying passenger is one of the unwanted things. When we hide, we slide, and the lamp of God goes out.

We move into the region, which is darker than beyond death. There was no hole in his pocket to make him impoverished, but there was a stone in his heart. That which should have been a token of abundance becomes the evidence of his poverty.

In your decline you will discover your real value

If you grant a man a gift, if you give any number of gifts to any number of people, you will discover how rich or poor their spirituality is. If you want to find out what this dove is like, send it to fly with a message, and it flies in the wrong direction. The Carrier Pigeon becomes a Homing Pigeon. Like the man in the parable of the talents with one talent, he took a 'nose dive', going into a full hole of problems. Doves always fly before the coming storms. They have the mentality of the escapist. There is no platform here for the escapologist. What you thought was so capable, so full and free, filled with such riches of grace turned out to be all pocket, all purse with no content. Like a shell lying on the beach with the pearl well removed. The echo of the sea you hear in the shell is not the sea at all. In the costs involved in serving God, we put lesser things in place of those values of real worth. One man said he would give the world to be like one great preacher, and, then, he asked what it would cost. The answer given was 'the world.' The very thing, which would have helped, was denied.

We can go backward and downward

The term 'backsliding' is an Old Testament phrase.[3] It is a picture, which is taken from the cow or heifer coming towards the altar. It can smell death, and hear the moaning of those who have gone before. There is blood and entrails on the floor; suddenly it realises its peril. It begins to slide in the free flowing blood backward away from the altar. As it moves by slithering stages, the altar and sacrifice become something in the dim future. That being afar off, now presents no challenge as the smell of sacrifice arises on the morning air. The very thing it was created for is being refused. As it goes backwards, it takes all its consecration with it. The fat representing the excellence of 1 Corinthians 13 is taken away with it. To go back from that which God requests, doesn't mean that we walk backwards. We just do our own thing, and forget what God has said to us. Jonah went forward, but it cost him dearly, apart from the spiritual aspect, it nearly cost him his life, the boat and all the crew. He just went in the opposite direction to what God had told him. That is refusing to use what you have been gifted with. To use a phrase of Jesus Christ, 'We go to war at our own charges.'[4] It costs far more to travel around in circles than go in a straight line. This expenditure of energy leaves you quite weak and frustrated. Many an arrow is lost as it falls short. The ones that are found and complete, are the ones that strike the target.

We descend into the smaller thing rather than the larger

He went for a smaller congregation in the Ship's Company. The ship was smaller than the city. The only richer and greater thing was the sea, which sought to destroy him. Sometimes in our denials, we reach for what we think are larger things, but they are really smaller. In clutching the forbidden we lose the grasp of His hand. Adam in the Garden of Eden with Eve reached for fruit of the tree, and touched its roots, thereby being buried with those roots.

He paid fully and dearly for his mistakes. He surrendered any largeness of heart he might have. His compassions failed, unlike the God of Jeremiah whose compassions fail not.[5] He lost obedience as a dog free from its lead.

Jonah's paying of his own fare was so small, as small as a mite, when it is compared with the peace he surrendered.

In the narrow spirit of refusal we lose the largeness of success and accomplishment in God. He could have been such a fine example. Just as great as what his name means: 'Dove of God', as the dove was which flew to Noah's ark with the olive branch in its beak. There is certain self-centredness here. He serves himself well. Those riches he has towards God are turned into poverty of the lowest poor house. In his poverty, he has too much to handle. Far better to walk with God, it is better and brighter than gold of Ophir. The full hand can be turned upwards, and then towards ourselves as we bless ourselves in all manners of ways.

The wasted years can beckon us with an empty hand

The Prodigal Son of Luke 15, wasted all his substance. Surely, this refers to more than goods. Didn't he waste his father's love and heart? Didn't he fritter away a deep fellowship and trust? He turned his back on his father, and that was worth more than anything he carried with him.

He might have gone out of the home, but he never went over the edge of the father's heart. It says in that parable that the elder brother was 'out' in the field (Twentieth Century New Testament) when he heard the music and dancing.[6] We can be in the field, and yet be so impoverished with a spirit of envy, jealousy, malice and pride, that we are as poverty stricken as the brother in the far country. When we are there the fatted calf becomes but a skeleton. Jonah commences as gold and degenerates into the dust of rust. He is robbed, as we are while day dreaming. While he is travelling in another direction, there are those journeying in the direction he should have gone, taking all the riches from that place of paved gold. Wherever he went once, he had denied God the right to be Lord and master, there was nothing added to him. He was not made richer, only poorer. Commencing in a place he concludes in the poor house. Having being seated among princes, he finds himself on the dung heap. Wait a while, and see the lovely bloom growing from that dung heap with Christ as the tender gardener. The prophet gave all he had. He did what he could, but not for God. If he had been saving for a rainy day, my, didn't it rain! Enough to accommodate a whale! Enough water for a ship to sail in. Enough water for him to sink in. God has to bring him to Psalm 23, wherein are contained the real riches of the talented person. Verse 4 'Though I walk through. You are with me', there is no 'with me' in the original language, it should read 'Though I walk through the valley of shadows, I will fear no evil, for you me', with nothing in-between. The 'are with' isn't there; it is only supplied to make the grammar acceptable.

That can happen without us perceiving it

It was the most expensive journey he would ever take. It was even more expensive than the journey from Jerusalem to Jericho that the Good Samaritan took, and fell among thieves.[7] He knew he had been robbed, but our problem is, sometimes we are robbed, and we know it not. Living off the beggarly elements of this world we think everyone else does the same. You can get so used to 'poverty of spirit' as this man did, that your margins of acceptability become very narrow. As Samson we seek to rise up and fight just as we have done in the past. We don't realise that the Spirit of the Lord has departed from us.[8]

You can pay your fare in full, and still go down, be down, feel down, and be left asleep in the side of the ship. There is a great swell in the heart when it becomes the investment of God, when you know you are doing what God has asked of you. We all need to be given to something larger than ourselves. The heart needs stretching or strengthening because what is heaven for! That is why the stars give themselves to the moon. That is why babies are given to mothers. The very large things are given not to overwhelm us but to minister greatness into us. We need new capacities daily that will challenge us. There is more up front! When it comes to the riches of God, do be a Scrooge. When it comes to the riches of this world, be as one totally satisfied. There is a cost in the currency of Christ, but those who give to the poor lend to the Lord.[9] That cost is not added up on a sheet, not part of a head for figures, it is not the delight of the Accountant. What we are involved in must not have Caesar's head stamped on it, for that speaks of works and human power. We operate by faith.

God will speak in many forms and fashions

One can imagine that in everything Jonah came to, there was that speaking voice. Each globule of water spoke a message. The creaking of the ship timbers would ask 'What are you doing here, Jonah the son of Amattai is found in Jonah 1:1. Jonah was the son of Amattai. Even the questions the sailors asked, the companions in the boat must have been as a dagger to the unbridled heart. The whole of his circumstance becomes one booming voice. He is as unmoved as the stone on the bottom of the sea. Here are your true riches in the virtue of His voice. One word used in Numbers 35:31, meaning 'satisfaction' is the Hebrew word atonement. It all comes from the cross. The cross and Calvary are God's bank and vault, where all the treasures of heaven are dispensed freely to the open hand.

As we travel with this man in his poverty, we touch seaweed and the bare boards of the ship. We move from blessing to basic existence. We reach the ocean bed. The inside of a whale has no adornment. There are no people there worth witnessing to. 'Davy Jones Locker' holds no gems of the first water. There is a certain loneliness about fishing. It becomes even worse when fish, fish for men, expressed in the fish swallowing Jonah.

He should have gone to Tarshish, the place of the fish. God certainly brought him to the place of fish in the sea. Note the size of the fish!

If talents are buried deep, you will become in God's Kingdom as the proverbial church mouse. It is so poor because it doesn't operate where the necessities of life are to be found in abundance.

You must discover and uncover your self

Pay your own fare, and go your own way. Long after he had spent his money from his pockets. Long after the last shekel or bottom dollar had gone if he dug deeper than riches or pocket, he would find his true self. If you go deeper, you must come and touch God. When the piles of pounds have gone, then we can begin to reach the realities of riches. As you touch God, there you will find the aptitudes you left behind, and the correct attitudes will be restored which both locusts and cankerworm have eaten.[10] Sometimes, we have to dig very deep to find the old love and passion of our first love for Jesus. You find it all where you left it. God marks the place with a cross.

The cost of rebellion gets higher and higher

When you seek to pay your way out of difficult situations with the carnal coinage of pretence, the costs get higher. It becomes as the fabled Greek books, which were offered for sale. If you didn't buy them when they were first offered, the next time the price had doubled. On each occasion, the price became higher. You can get lost in the cost of living. To be 'bankrupt' is to have a broken bench where the carpenter of Nazareth cannot work. There is no place for Him. He has promised us the Bread of Life, the true manna, sometimes the real cost is what we seek to put upon that bread. It can and will cost far more to hide your gift than use it. One is so easy, the other so difficult, but we always choose, as a matter of human nature, the more obstinate.

We do shun our responsibilities and share our disabilities

Jonah paid for his passage, and then he sailed under the pirate's flag hiding yet hoisting it from the mainsail. There was no responsibility in what he did. Let others do all the sailing and guiding. I will take a sleep in my poverty. As the snail, I will go into my shell, while the world passes by. He threw the responsibility for himself on others. He was there for the ride. He was in it for what was in it. He wasn't here to contribute but to commute. That is a token of our bankrupt nature, when we leave all the toil and sweat to others of lesser talents than we have.

Let the oar do the rowing! It was going to be a pleasure cruise. God had other ideas. The riches of God were going to come again in a prepared wind, storm, fish, gourd and worm. God can turn our sleep into a dream of new things. When we do as this servant, we occupy barren ground, uncultivated. We are as an orchestra of instruments, reduced to a trumpet solo. We are that choir; the voices numberless as they are in the book of Revelation, but it is all reduced to a solo. We have lost it, and which was clothed becomes unclothed.

We can make the wrong choices

If a man comes with outer adornment, which is rich in colour, we choose that one, but God chooses the abundance of the heart, for from this the mouth speaks. It was the heart of the prophet which dictated a narrow spirit, sectarian at least, and denominational at most. It was as a bell with only one note, forever peeling but never appealing.

Jonah became as the ship, without wares. Going but going nowhere. Going but going with nothing. Nothing to take with him and nothing to bring. Poor indeed, for as the ship had been fully laden, it was now quite empty, as an image of the prophet who travelled on it? Your very circumstances can become a mirror of your soul. Reflecting what you are or what you are not. It is not the size of the box, but the content, which will count and bring shouts of glee when it is opened before the eyes of great and small.

There can be the multiplication of loneliness and emptiness.

This holy book illustrates the Parable of the Talents in Matthew 25, after being left with the one talent, nothing is taken from it, and nothing is added to it. It is as it was at the beginning. From beginning to ending, there is nothing in between. There is the shadow of poverty over the face of it.

The total cost of going it elsewhere is to go alone. Even in this, God slides in through our loneliness, and makes emptiness into something more than fullness, into usefulness. As the ship sails the sea, so he must go for God. We will sink, if the centre of His will is pulled out.

C. H. Spurgeon wrote 'Jonah lost the presence of God. He lost his sense of the love of God. He lost the faithfulness of God. He lost his comfort of God. He lost his time because he still had to go to Nineveh.' Here was a born winner who became a dying loser. All we ever do in our poverty is to delay what God will do. There is the delaying of the coming spring in the grasp of winter. We simply lengthen the race, but we don't alter the purposes of God. He found that there is no fatted calf away from home. There is no richness of music and the sure smile of father's face. That, which began to be merry, only began to be merry, but it didn't continue until the final curtain was lowered. He came to that experience they came to at the wedding in Cana of Galilee.[11] They had no wine. The difference is they told Jesus, and He did something about it. He put some of His red joy into the water and turned it into wine. Either that or it saw its Creator and blushed.

There can be emptiness in the poverty of spirit

When an empty ship is going to Tarshish, the man who is empty goes with it. Birds of a feather flock together. There are two of a kind, here. Matthew Henry, the Puritan writer records 'The ready way is not always the right way.' We need to ask many questions, and one of these is where will it lead to? It led him to almost be like those in the New Testament, who made 'shipwreck' of their faith. On some of the old maps of Jamaica it is written 'The Land of Looking Back'. These words were written, because escaped slaves knew that the soldiers would follow them to recapture and enslave them. It became known as 'The Land of Looking Back.' This wayward traveller could say I have been, I have seen, but I have done nothing. Jonah had no watchfulness to offer. No deep devotion is offered to us. He has no word such as the apostle offered in a storm: 'I believe God.' When we read this story, it is no love affair. There is nothing in the moment we might take up and use. He has been no pioneer; he has blazed no trail because of the cost of a talent denied.

Notes

1	2 Corinthians 10:4	5	Lamentations 3:22	9	Proverbs 19:17
2	Proverbs 11:24	6	Luke 15:25	10	Joel 2:25
3	Hosea 4:16	7	Luke 10:30-37	11	John 2:2
4	Luke 14:31	8	Judges 16:20		

CHAPTER 7
The talent broken and sinking

When the ship started to flounder, all on board and all part of it, including Jonah with his many sided talent, meaning all things to no one, its many properties from God were sinking too. It is recorded, 'The ship was likely to be broken.'[1] The term 'broken' can mean 'broken hearted.' it can also mean 'to see things differently' that is the way God wanted him to see them. To see and to know is the end of all argument and friction. It can be the beginning of a new agreement birthed in understanding another's point of view. The wind may touch us on the outside but there is that within which needs to be removed. He knows where we respond the best. His touch is the key but there are lots of them within His scales. Isaiah 61:1, where the same word used in Jonah is given as 'broken' is used means 'to be rubbed to the heart.' It is used in the New Testament in Luke 4:18 of those who are 'bruised.' It was more than the sinking of the vessel that the Master of the Ocean was requiring. He was seeking to rock Jonah out of his lethargy.

It is not the way we commence but conclude

Many a young person, gifted and graced by God has commenced ministry with the sun shining as if it would never set again, but to find their faith marooned along with other abilities in foul weather. There are certain islands, which are not the real destination at all, but they find themselves marooned there.

When things don't degenerate all together or immediately, and a rock doesn't come crashing out of the sky, making us dash for cover, we assume that everything is all right. God begins to work on that surrounding us, and what He does is that we might be brought out of that small place of security, and learn to swim and face greater depths. Even if you shake milk long enough in a bottle, as the creator rocked the prophet in a boat, it will turn into cheese. God has His own time, and the type of challenge, which will move us, so that out of the depths we cry to the Lord. Yet, even the things around us will acknowledge that there is something wrong. Does there need to be the appearance a ship with broken planks of timber before we are aware that all is not well, and this is not just another cruise down the river. Jonah would discover himself in those circumstances surrounding him. The broken bits of the ship, if it went that far, could be used as the rungs of the ladder to climb, carrying his talents, and placing all back into the heart of God.

God reveals His heart to us in our pain

Each groan of the ship's timbers become echoes of the heart of God, and the pain it feels while we are in the ship. We might be sailing, but we really are adrift and going to the bottom and not the top. The rocky bottom was facing him, suggesting he was coming to the end of himself, but he had hardly come to the beginning of God. Somewhere in those dark waters, there was that seeking to help him with his endowment. God had to break the wooden cage to release the singing bird. As the wooden ship was battered. He needed to be brought to the largest place with the most freedom to express all his riches in God. He was involved in drifting as found in Hebrews 2:1, 'Lest we drift away.' It is a nautical figure of a vessel with its mooring loosened, and it is drifting. Maybe it is drifting towards the rocks of a reef. There is no plan; there isn't any call for your gifts as you drift.

Mark the fact, that after paying his own fare, even though captain and crew are working at it, all the ceremonies and rituals are right, he is drifting. It is towards what is feared, felt or seen. The hand of God is beyond all he can see. The God that would save Nineveh would bring the man and his rarities to rise again, to get back on track.

When we step out - God steps in

God stepped in and we have that around him turned into a foaming sea, the roaring and howling wind. Mad prophet, person of God, God is calling! His calling card is a very destructive wind. He destroys to build. He steps in not to crush with His feet, but to make a way in the sea. There are three things that the sailors did cast out of the ship. They cast out wares.[2] They cast lots.[3] They cast the exile out of the boat.[4] When it says 'they did cast out' the same word is used in Jonah chapter 1:4 of God sending a strong wind. It is describing the throwing of a spear to strike its target. Guess who the target was? As all the strength of the sailors was in that one act of throwing him over board, so the strength of the Almighty was in and behind all the activity of the sea. It wasn't to break the talent but to shape it and make it more effective. The lifeboat was the hand of Mercy. The hand of God is safer than any maritime vessel, no matter how sea worthy.

When we lose sight of God everything becomes too much

The called one couldn't handle what God had granted him. He was about to be thrown as some stone into the depths of the sea. He could muster his own fare, but he couldn't take care of that from God. It became like a ship in a storm. Power was unleashed as some weapon formed in the winds, that immeasurable by men, and just as uncontrollable. God will shove and push, toss and pitch what we are leaning on. He went down to sleep, but God shakes the bed. He is trying to remake Jonah, as a person would re-make a bed. All his pillows are arranged by God's billows, and all are neat, tidy and 'Bristol fashion' the sheets are shaken into shape. Somewhere in that bed a talent is buried. From the bed there was a requirement for healing and wholeness to arise. There has to be a new man stepping out of this bed of clothes, wearing, not night apparel, but that given by God for adornment. He is clothed in missionary clothes that are the clothes of the heart. Healing and wholeness is taken on board as crewmembers. Note the wind sent by God didn't have to pay its fare.

Circumstances are changed to change us

Circumstances do alter dramatically, when God begins to huff and puff; He blows the house down whether it is made of clay, wood, stone or stubble. There had to be the taking on board of a greater cargo. This boat became the carpenter's workshop. It was rather like a theatre stage, and guess who the main player is? He is in danger of being broken with the ship. God breaks to take out of the resistant stone, that the golden vein might appear. God will blow us off course to blow us on course. All that we wrap our prize in will be removed. Would the wind fan into a flame the dying embers? Was this the day of the Phoenix?

We can lack the presence and power of the Lord

The presence of the Lord was the thing lacking. That presence was lacking in the runaway's character. We can have the gifts of God, without having the Giver of that enabling. We can travel light, but without the true light of care and love. The Spirit of the Lord departed from Samson and he didn't know it.[5] He had lost his faculty of recognition. From that first gentle voice we have now a strong resisting voice which reigns supreme. From the gentle tap and still small voice we have a buffeting wind, that is as wild as a boxer in the first round. God has been training for all eternity. Poor Jonah has had no training for reigning. He is so short of wind! The Supreme has all the wind He requires for tiring the prophet. He wants him to come up gasping for the wind, the air of the Almighty. Grandparents took a child to the seaside. While they were there, they met an old friend, who grumbled about everything and anything. Nothing seemed to be welcomed by him. All was wrong. When he left, the child asked what was wrong with him. Making an excuse for him the Grandparents said 'He is not well, we think he is suffering from sunstroke.' The child replied 'I do hope that none of you ever have a sunset!'. While ever we are not the owner of the boat, the seas, wind and sky they have many willing helpers. They will readily take on a task, and show us how reluctant we are. Have you ever thought when the sun shines, what a brilliant work the sun is doing for its Creator? Here, it was wind, rain, storm, waves, wet and groaning timbers; all became part of God's marching army. They are going to take back what has been stolen. They are going to chase and chasten somebody. There is a pirate on board this vessel. He is a stowaway from God. He had taken his talent into this wooden tank, this weapon of the water, and it had become a coffin for his varieties.

We require more than our emotions touching

Sailors always spoke of ships as if they had feelings. It was about to be broken. To them, it had hopes and fears, emotions and a heart. It had longings and hopes, almost like a human being. They said a ship could speak, cry, weep and call. Let this ship be called 'Discovery.' May there be the discovery of new worlds. That craft ready to be broken, let it be saved. It can be rebellion that we sail on. It can be our own wills, wanting to do it our way. It is indeed a very salty sea when we do not surrender to God.

God makes us cry that we might sail to safety even on our tears. The hurt can be that carrying us from the battle injured, to be placed at the feet of Jesus for healing and informing. The wind of God came to snatch back that belonging to its Creator. In Acts 2, the wind came before the fire. The wind came before they went everywhere, preaching the word of God. Not only the ship needs to be broken; there is a requirement for a shattered self. Some parts of our lives need to be buried at sea, and then we need to place a sign there saying 'No fishing here!' God wants to reduce your ship of knowledge, good works, fair words and leaning to be just a simple thing, retaining what He has given as you come out of your circle of pain.

Let us come back to the cross

Back to just faith, just grace, and just my gift, to the wood of His cross. When they carried water from the well in a bucket there was one safe way of stopping it from spilling. They used to place a piece of wood in the water. The Cross of Christ does that for us. There you will find God's child as He intended him to be. Wrapped up in the love of a Father. The covered must be uncovered. A reeling ship unlocks all doors. No locks remain locked. In Acts 16:27, when God moved all the doors were opened. God breaks it down and brings it down to what we can handle. He was asleep, so the next step into death would have been easy. God could say what the Roman Centurion said when he found the man on guard asleep, and killed him with his sword. 'I left him as I found him!'

Why is adversity allowed?

The one and only reason things happened was to get him out of his inertia; out of the deep, out of his sleep. The sleeping figure was as a fish in a net, and he didn't realise it was so full of himself, that at any moment, it was likely to break. Complacency can be a large coat drawn around us as a bed sheet. In all this the very purpose of his existence and calling were being made sure. There should have been a tying down with cords of love; things ready to be swept overboard. With the wind, God was knocking all the loose nails back into the timbers of his character. God required him to take a reading. Have a look at the spiritual map called the bible. Take a reading from that compass called the cross.

That presence is still with you, holding you

Twice we are told that he rose up to flee from the presence of the Lord. Yet, that very presence can be a matter of interpretation. When he didn't feel the presence of the One who called him, that presence was there. The very trouble was God's throne. The very noises around him were the voice of God speaking from the deep, into the depth of his heart. That presence can be in wind, waves, storms and all manners of happenings. When we are not feeling His presence, maybe, it is, so that we should at that time be listening for His voice. You can't hear what He is saying if your ears are stuffed with bed blankets, and the sheets are over your eyes to prevent you seeing the real happenings around you. He went into bed, and being asleep, he was shrouded in mystery. You cannot get away from that which was always there. God peeping at you through the stars. God laughing with you in the sunshine. God speaking through the thunder. Looking at the sea and thinking God is larger and deeper than this! Even in the violence and even in the whispering of the wind there is a voice. God wanted to get him as deep into His nature as the boat was in the water, and as deep as the whale. When he came into the presence of Jehovah he could bring all that God had deposited with him. God will blow with His wind to blow out the rebellion of the heart the size of any great fish. When God knocks on the door, He does it sometimes from the outside, and those knocks are rather loud. Seeking to move the walls of the ship which were between the man and his Lord. It is not to destroy us, but to simply break us open, so that rare jewel deposited can fall again at God's feet to have some more shaping and polishing done to it. There are new facets in the old stone. He comes through all openings in a gust of wind. That used by Noah had pitch placed between the planks of wood to keep the waters at bay. No matter how tightly we seal things, or resist, we shall never keep God at a distance and seal Him out of our lives.[6]

God uses natural things for spiritual reasons

Maybe the wind blew, not to blow the house down, but to get Jonah to close a few windows, for through them many things had escaped. God used the most natural things for the most spiritual reasons. God never blows us off our feet. What is sent is meant to blow us back on our feet. If we are blown down, it is while we are down we might find what we have dropped in the rush to get away from true love. The term 'wind' means to blow, to breathe, to blast.[7] It is a figure of anger. It is the broom making a clean sweep. Watch the autumn wind do its cleansing work as it tosses leaves from their perches! The same word used for 'wind' is translated 'Spirit'. The Spirit of mercy and truth can be a convincing, convicting Spirit. God uses all of heaven to get a heavenly disposition into us. God using His best gifts to enable us to use what has been granted to you. See the soul under conviction as that lashed by the sea. It dips down, and then when you think it has disappeared forever, it reappears as something freshly baptised in water. All this and more to get his aptitudes back up on top. As he sleeps, so does everything he is in God. Sleep, spiritual sleep can stuff the ears with dullness until one voice and one act of righteousness following us can sound like another. We can be as wooden as the ship that was sailing, and as unconcerned as the person asleep. He was meant to be tossing and turning. That activity was part of the plan by God. When God makes your bed you are not going to sleep easily!

God wants to bind you to Himself forever

Using the wind and waves as ropes He wants to bind us to Him forever. The wind can be as the whirring of the potter's wheel, but what a difficulty we witness here, getting the clay onto that wheel.

The wind didn't arise by chance. The One who was supposed to be served raised it up, using all the might of heaven to toss this little matchbox to and fro. The hand of Power moves around the heart of the gifted person, not wanting to break, for sometimes it is a lifting hand, a cheering hand, a comforting hand, but even a stirring and chastening hand. He makes the sea flow in and out of that same hand. Jonah, God is using His gifts for you, why not use your gifts for Him? That hand was bigger and stronger than the ship, sea or whale. Note, while he was asleep, the hand worked. While the model lies in the clay, the best work is done. From that man-made wreck of a thing, there needs to emerge from the splinters that moving into the hand, which acts as a covert in the time of storm. We need to recover and be refreshed so that we might continue. God has another ship in mind in the shape of His hand that we might enter into for safety.

There are many warning notices

Job 28:25 tells us that God uses the wind to build on. He blows away the old and builds the new. The wind was both chilling, calling and compelling. 'The Lord sent',[8] it does bring us to the suggestion that He sent, like a man will send his voice to warn a child, tottering towards the precipice. The same word 'sent' is used of the javelin being thrown in 1 Samuel 18:11. God did some fishing, using the wind and the storm as a rod. He takes all the happenings of your life, all the hurt and pain with the broken strands, and weaves them into a net, to bring us into the shore of His security and surety. The Lord's given graces must be rescued. The investments of the Holy One are in this life. God is seeking to break the ship, but it is only with the design that the golden contents might spill out. To get the real nature out, shake the bottle! Take the lid off it! When the grape is crushed, there is the potential for wine. When the alabaster slate is broken, the ointment fills the whole house.[9] What was restricted in a small phial now fills the house.

God sends that we might throw. The word 'sent' is used twice in relation to Jonah 1:4,5,12. It is used of 'throwing things' overboard. You may cast all your cares on Him. Lay those cares as sick people at His feet or as they put the clothes on the donkey for Jesus to ride on. The word used in 1 Peter 5:7, 'cast' is the same Greek word, 'epirrhipto,' is used for laying the sick down, and placing clothes on a donkey's back. Seat Him on your difficulty and all will be made whole. Many things were thrown out, but the best thing was not brought to the surface, the very enabling that would take him to his destination. God doesn't huff and puff for nothing, there is a blowing to bend and shape. Small seeds of great variety are carried along by the wind to be planted by the same wind. The wind that carries is the wind that blows, and the same wind that blows sows seeds in a better and richer field. What has been a wilderness waste, suddenly blossoms as the almond tree. There is certain pollination as the wind blows. We have heard of 'trade winds', this was God's. Trading with and training the heart. Seeking to get the merchantman trading with his pearls.

There are times when the soul needs to catch up with the body.

The Japanese people have a phrase, which says 'The body is waiting for the soul to catch up with it.' The prodigal Son 'came to himself' as one who had been in a faint or in a sleep.[10] Step from the past and into the future, now! That wind can become all manners of instruments, taking on all manners of shapes. If we need to step up, it will become that step. If the talent needs renewing, then it will become a renewing wind. The wind reigns wherever it will. Its throne is established right where he was. That rebellious nature must face an antidote in wind just as strong.

A new chapter can begin as the page is turned

A new chapter could begin as the old is blown off the page. A new light can shine when the old light is extinguished by the wind. Extinguished light can become distinguished light in love for the Master of the matter. This ship contains a cargo in the gifts of the man from Gath, which the ship's captain was unaware of.

When a fog at sea held up one of God's servants, and it meant he would be late for his appointment, he simply knelt by the captain's table, and asked God to help him to be on time for his appointment. A strong wind suddenly blew, as it did on the Spanish Armada, in English history of their wars with Spain, and the fog lifted. The servant of God arrived on time. As he believed, so it was and ever shall be. Following the storm the calm of His presence. There is an eye of the storm where perfect peace reigns. One family was travelling to Australia, and the sea was very rough. They had with them a young child, who was aged three. She said she wanted to console her seasick mother. 'I will sing to you', she said. She began to sing an old chorus 'Row me over the Tide.' That is human comfort and consolation, and, sometimes it can make matters worse. The best has yet to be for you and this seer.

Notes

1	Jonah 1:4	5	Judges 16:20	9	Mark 14:3
2	Jonah 1:5	6	Genesis 6:14	10	Luke 15:17
3	Jonah 1:7	7	Jonah 1:4		
4	Jonah 1:12,15	8	Jonah 1:4		

CHAPTER 8

The prayer offered about your talent

There comes a moment, when we are in difficult situations that a new ship needs to sail from within our problem. It is that called 'All Prayer'. God will allow us time to pray and wait. 'The King of Kings' comes to help us in our infirmity. That broken and torn by disappointment is healed by His presence.

Beginning to trust God and pray can be so small, almost the size of a grain of sand, yet, through prayer and communication it can grow into something immeasurable. It is a matter of saying to Jehovah 'Don't you care if I perish?' The sure thing is at that split second, split to allow you time to pray, we begin to realise that the answer was not afar off, but nearer than we thought. It is so close that it has become as acceptable as the clothes we wear, and the air we breathe. There is that familiarity, and that lack of knowledge, turning what is the latest answer to prayer into that forgotten as something swept out to sea.

We must call to God in 'the nick of time'

We must call in the 'time of need', just in the 'nick of time.'[1] The old Hebrew proverb says 'Some doors are open, some are closed, but the door of prayer is always open.' You can cry between the creaks of the planks of wood, and you can cry between the waves. Each wave is meant to wash away your old ideas of God, and to bring in a whole new concept as the tide rushing in, not controlled by the moon but by the Son. Even the fish of the sea send 'sound echoes' through the waves and each sound, like a rubber ball bounces off the wave and the rock until it reaches its destination. So is prayer for us, when talents need keeping afloat.

There are times when I have to be goaded into praying.

The Master of the vessel had to goad them all into prayer.[2] He acted not only as captain of the ship but also as the priest. With strong language, as strong as any whip he seeks to put the slaves to the work of their taskmaster. Prayer will save you from sinking, and will set you thinking. It lifts higher than the waves and plunges deeper than the coral. Right thoughts will enter into your mind about yourself. That realistic will be applied to your heart as a 'yard stick'. Sometimes, before the prayer reaches the front of the mouth, or the top of the mind, God will have answered. At other times, the answer to a prayer is as long as it takes the small irritation in the shell of the oyster to become a pearl. It can take as long for God to answer as it does the sea to grind that rock into sand, and little by little it becomes so large until a child fills a bucket with it and makes a sandcastle. If God doesn't answer straight away, it means that He needs you to grow bigger in the lashing of the seas around you. The lashing waters might bind you, but not the prayer of the one you pray to. This is the mould shaping the mouth that utters the prayer. That around you is working on the heart until it is filled with longing for God. You need your gifting raising from the ocean bed, as some long sunken wreck. The heart accepting its uniqueness in that granted by the One who is more than a storm. Why that awful trouble, that designed to design you, is only as a man raking the garden soil! There needs to be that given to you in the Bread of Heaven that which will feed you now and evermore, making you strong and able to sustain your enabling. There was a need for something more than waves and seaweed to come out of this storm. We don't want to come through with just wind whistling in our ears, and bits of broken plank or plankton stuck in our ears. There will be lots of broken bits, but we need that which is as whole as that which is complete. We must not come out as we went in. A lick of paint will not alter the design of the ship or increase its capacity to cope with storms. The 'plimsoll line' may be placed higher or lower, but we still need to come through to our destination.

We sleep when we should watch and pray

What Jonah is and all that made him a man, is within his grasp. Every talent that Jehovah Nissi had granted him was there to make him into that man of God. What the sea does with rocks and anything thrown into it, prayer will do with our problems. The best way to learn how to pray is to pray. There was a time to pray, and this was the time. A talent was being wasted.

Awake oh sleeper! Commit afresh your graces into the hands of the Awakened. I was raised in a mining area of Yorkshire, where there was a man, who came around to arouse all those who had over slept. He was quaintly called 'A Knocker Up.' He used to bang on the door until the light was switched on, and he heard a voice responding from within. His bangs on the door were turned into surly words from the sleeper. There is that needing to be fished from these swirling waters of the mind. In the dark places development of exciting times can take place. There can be the developing of sunshine in a prayer answered. Prayer will always be you asking, begging, pleading, and God answering. It is Jehovah Jireh's hand being placed into your bowl. Your deficiency is met in His sufficiency. You have to get down to get up. You must awake to appreciate. It is this pleading prayer, stronger than the waves around you that takes some of the salt out of the swim. It brings to an acknowledgement of what we have in Elohim.

There is always a way out through prayer

A life raft can go out in a prayer, until we see a into a calmer and deeper place. Taking you from pain to peace. When ships are sinking, rocket flares are sent out. The SOS 'save our souls' is sent to anyone who will readily respond. What we are in our hearts travels in our prayers. The broken, the hurt, the sleep, the apathy and that lethargic spirit of the sleeper needs committing to the Keeper. There comes the crisis causing you to call upon Him who called you. Prayer is calling back to God who has already called on you. It is the confession that this is too deep for the shallow thoughts of your mind.

Through prayer we leave the ground of neutrality. Whatever that ability is, prayer can leave it enthroned in heavenly splendour. It can take those things around us, and weave them into something better than seaweed or waves. They can be taken and used for our good. The sunken treasure which is the ability to pray, fast bound in the bottom of your heart.

Your prayer can be your rope ladder

The Ship's Master is the 'captain of the rope', for so his name suggests. He was the one who used the ropes to under gird the ship while it was passing through a storm, hence the word 'frappings', given as 'helps' in the New Testament.[3] He used these ropes to bind and loose with. He stood there with the ropes in one hand to give him balance as the ship sways to and fro. He uses it almost like the bird on its perch. To have the ropes in his hand gave him a sense of comfort and authority. That likely to be swept over board was held intact with a hand of rope. He knew how to stop things lurching with the ship, and rolling from side to side. It was his ability with the rope to see to all these things. There was no knot which he couldn't tie for safety. That rope could soon be turned into a rope ladder, and escape was always possible through his manipulations of the rope. He used what he had, just as you need to use what you have for God. There was the rope to which the sheet anchor was attached. There was a certain rope for the capstan when in port. It was this same man that called them to pray. Prayer can be the master of the rope. It can do everything that this master did. What rope was to captain and the ship, giving it more security, prayer can be as this rope to you. Your gift from God might have degenerated into a piece of old rope, where once it was a silver thread or a cord using it to bind the sacrifice. The ends of it can be frayed. Yet, Jehovah can still take it and use it, as we are aroused out of our sleep. We can be made larger with the love of God. Bound to Him, drawn as a rope is pulled towards His heart of love. Bringing us so close that we look at Him rather than the problem. When we see it all through the one, we shall do valiantly.

God has many ways of answering prayer

God could have sent a shark to devour the man. That would have been the end of the matter. God would have closed the book. He is not for closing it, there is lots more He wants to write. Dipping the pen into our failures, He writes our successes. He could have sent a swordfish to saw the man, who doesn't pray in two. He could have made a better Jonah out of the one bad half than the two, making him into the prophet of God. There could have been some great catastrophe, ready to spring on board this ship, and eat it away board-by-board and nail-by-nail. It could have been as some ghostly ship, sailing on in the night with no one on board, lights left on and half eaten meals left untouched. God sent a man with a message for men. If only Jonah had been as conscientious as this ship's director was to his duty, and the owners of the vessel.

Prayer can bring us into line with the mind of God

It is prayer that can bring us into line, the line that God has made. It is what the mind of the Almighty requires. It is anchoring us in His will. God doesn't always answer prayer straight away. What a large answer, the size of a whale! Some prayer! Some answer! He waits for us to grow as large as possible in our hearts, that as the sea was large enough to handle Jonah and the whale, we are big enough and mature enough, to rise above that shoving us down. Having enough salt in our veins to be able to handle the difficult and the nasty side of life. Having come through, we have learned to pray, and how to handle that given to us be it a ship, a worm or whale.

God answers, sometimes, before we call. Before the dawn breaks, the prayer is answered that was offered during the night. It can take as long as the river flows and the sun shines. It might be offered in darkness but the answer can be received with the morning light. Prayer can be offered in that resembling a sea swell, but the answer comes in peace. What was sent up in trouble would return as that twisted and knotted formed into a beautiful pattern. The pattern for living needs to be found. Only the Master of the Sea can knit waves of water into patterns for Jonah to realise that God's throne is there in it with him.

Prayer will only be what we let God make it

Prayer brings us back from the brink of the brine. It brings a dead deposit into something living and vital. It becomes, once again, as we pray what it was created to be. Let the sail be the sail, let the rudder be the rudder, and let the gifting of God be free, as free as the bird flying overhead. The waves are beating the message on the side of the ship. Let what is God's go, setting it free to bless others with. Let it sing as the bird with a song. Don't let this become a destination or a goal when it was meant to be a breathing space, so that all the salt of the sea could brace the prophet for future happenings. What travelling in the waters does to the outward appearance, Jonah required it to happen in his heart. There could be a new shape, and a new look, there.

There needs to be stirrings, not only in the sea, with its great billow waves. There must be stirrings where the faculty is buried deep. It is more than covered by seaweed or circumstances. The sea can never bury what it has given us, unless we require it to do so. Praying where you are, gets you to where you should be, rather than where you want to be. In the will of the infinite, is a finely furnished ship with all crew correct and present. To be outside of the will is just a floating raft, going nowhere, very slowly. Who wants to be a floating carcass? Who would desire to be seaweed adrift? There is much rubbish tossed up on the beach, as if the sea has a great hand for taking rubbish and dumping it. This prayer is another member needing to be added to the crew. It is the extra hand, and another spanner for the nut. It is a fresh wind for the sails, driving us onward.

We must pray to the God of the situation

They were exhorted to call upon their god. The gods were carved into the prow of the ship. As the ship submerged under the waters, and then arose on the next wave, they breathed a sigh of relief. Their god had defeated that wave He might not defeat the next one. They made gods of different happenings. They were now fishing for a god to fit into this storm at sea. Would their gods see them through this? It was at this moment you discovered what a man's god was. If that god or coincidence helped, that god would become known as 'the god who brings through a storm.' It would become the flavour of the month. To call upon El Shadai, as Jonah should have done would have meant that not only the ship was saved, but that received from above would be revealed in the midst of a storm. Half the battle wasn't the raging sea it was the buried bit. God doesn't always give you what you ask. Jonah couldn't handle his talents. God can handle all things. A man asked God, and said, 'Lord, what are a million years to you?' The Lord answered, 'Only a second.' The man said, 'And what are a million pounds to you?' 'Only a penny,' God replied. 'Give me a penny?' the man said. And God said 'Just a second.'

God will arouse us to pray

The storm and all that happening around could shake a ship, it could toss it like a cork, but this man is asleep, unmoved by it all. God was shaking him to see if that in his pockets or secreted in his heart might fall out to be claimed. If the cork is taken from the neck of the bottle, what will come out? Asleep in a wooden coffin that was floating on the sea. You can't write an epitaph on water. There would be no history or proclamation about his life.

Jonah is still asleep, lethargy and apathy are stuffed in his ears.[4] It does say fast, asleep (the comma is mine). The wax of his old letters has set hard where he needs to hear the voice of God. The sent one is asleep.

70

The God that 'neither slumbers nor sleeps' did not send him to sleep. The gentle rocking of a self well-being did it. The word 'asleep' describes a soldier, going into his tent, after a weary battle and going to sleep, the sleep of a baby. After wrestling in battle, he sleeps. The Jacob in Jonah has been wrestling with God. There is only one winner, and it is neither sea, ship or whale. The word 'asleep' is taken from a word meaning to 'stun'. It describes a 'slothful son.' He has been stung by his own conscience, and betrayed by those of his own kind. Only Jonah sleeps. Only Jonah is running a race with a deep drop at the end of it. While he sleeps, prayer is awake. It puts the hand back into the hand of God. It seals the ship with tar. We lower the true anchor when we call upon the Lord. The colours hoisted tell that we are registered in heaven. We are part of the Colony of Heaven. You must awake, not to the captain, but to God. In place of his rough and uncouth words, you have the gentle whisperings of God. You must meet with that at the other end of the calling voice. There is a lifeboat, lifebuoy and lighthouse when we utter our deepest longings. They are more able to preserve you than the salt preserves the fish or the rotting carcass.

Prayer lifts the burden from us

It is this sort of utterance removing the sickness of denial from us. 'Is any afflicted among you? Let him pray', James 5:13. When we look to see what has lifted us we see a hand, and into it fits all the oceans of the world. I remember how my mother used to stick knitting needles into the partially knitted garment to stop it falling part. We have to suffer like that sometimes. It stops us taking our talent and having a funeral service arranged for it. It can and will remove the diseases from the heart. The ship's ruler asks, 'What ails you?' Here is more discolour in the character of Jonah than in his face, brought there by the turbulent sea. God will think upon us when we pray. That is strange theology! We are in the heart of Shalom, and not just in the mind. We are part of His works. He will re-arrange all the waves. He becomes the compass, to bring us back to where the map, the Bible says we should be. Prayer is more than a shout or a noise. It is not a squeak. It is heard far above all the noises of other things. Nothing sounds better in heaven than the prayer of a repentant man. All the discord becomes concord. A concord of delight, as much as the setting sun is to a labouring man. Which is the best port for the ship carrying the man with the ability to come into? It is that represented by prayer. This cargo is better than gold or silver. Unlike the ships of France, where the people were pleading for bread, and were promised it, but when the ships arrived, they only had cargoes of sand. A thing given can degenerate into something quite useless if we let it!

God's favours are found in prayer

If we pray, the leader of this importune* prayer meeting says, God will 'favour' us.[5] The Chaldee (This is the Chaldean Version of the Old Testament Scriptures.) says 'God will be merciful to us.' The word for 'favour' is shine, it describes a piece of shining metal. When we have no ability to chop through or go through, God will provide the metal. God is metal among wood. What was required from the runaway was that restored which had been stolen and put to sleep in him. Prayer can be the opening of the door, just wide enough for us to see the light on the other side of it. It can be God showing us the first rung of the ladder.

When prayer doesn't work, and the situation is just as it was before, only more so, then they resort to a new thing. In modern parlance, they had a raffle, and Jonah received the winning ticket. He drew the short straw. The winning number was his, but like many winning the National Lottery, he found that winning is losing. The reason none of these things moved him was because he was asleep to One thing, and therefore, to everything. If we are asleep, drawing our talent over our heads like a warm sheet on a cold winter's night, God can do all the shouting, saying, speaking and drawing, while we do all the sleeping. Jonah answered not a snore! All the designs of God merged into a scribble. The response of the man is as the scribbling of a child on some wooden plank. He was asleep to his God. He had closed eyes to his loss. Unaware of the storm, the boat had become a rocking chair. Whichever way the storm rocked him, he simply got back into bed on the wrong side. When the New Testament missionary was shipwrecked, he called upon the Lord. It didn't save him from shipwreck; it saved him from being a wreckage in life.[6] It gave him an opportunity to preach, and the Island of Malta heard the Gospel for the first time, many were healed and set free. God closes one door and opens ten.

---

* Importune means 'that hastily arranged'. To press urgently with troublesome application. That which is troublesome. It is anything of difficult access. The word importune comes from the Latin, 'importunus' meaning 'not an harbour'.

Praying is leaving your calling card with God

To pray is to leave your calling card with God. It is being sensible enough to know that you should pray about it. It says that because Jesus was on board, as the ship sailed, it was suddenly at the land where they were going. To ask is to arrive. To pray is to dig deep, until that buried by years is yet to be bathed in tears. That in the darkness, entombed in a ship can still see the light of day. Praying is the shining of another light that we stumble not. It is walking in the light as He is in the light.

Someone was asked to present any needs they might have for prayer. The lady said, "I would like you to pray for my key-ring, I have lost it - anyone who finds it will know it is mine, because written on it are the words 'Have you talked with the Lord, today?'" The American Indians met together to discuss prayer, and how God answers prayer. They said that when they prayed for healing it worked twenty five percent of the time. When they prayed for rain, it worked fifty percent of the time, but when they prayed that the sun would rise, it worked all the time!

When two minister's wives met at the sewing class, they were discussing the work that their husbands were doing in their respective churches. Our church is so poor the church mouse was seen leaving with an empty bag. It we have another split or more trouble, we are so small, it will result in a funeral. That's strange said the other wife, my husband is so happy, and blessed of God. The work is growing. Our situation changed radically when my husband had a mirror placed at the front of the church. He asked those who wanted to know who it was holding the church back from making progress, to come and look in the mirror, and God would reveal to them as they looked, who it was. 'That is wonderful', replied the downhearted minister's wife. They continued the sewing., the wife of the one with so many problems was mending the seat of his trousers. The wife of the one with so much blessing, was mending the holes in the knees of his trousers.

Prayer can open all closed doors

Prayer can open all things, bend all things, and heal all things. It can stand a prophet, looking outward and forward, as he should have been doing. It can put him and you back on course. It restores the borrowed time and wasted years.

'Let him cry upon his god.' The word cry is what the overseer uses. It is the tear of a prayer, which moves God, and takes you out of the sea, and into a smaller river. Into something that you can manage. Jonah, remember, had bought himself, and brought himself into all this. Every wave, every grain of sand and salt, he had paid for it dearly. The exhortation is to fix your self to some great power. Prayer is the golden hinge on the door of opportunity. A man wanting to scale great heights calls for boot spikes and ropes with grappling hooks. The person who is thirsty and wanting refreshment calls for a drink. He calls for liquid re-invigoration. The person who wants to paint calls for his paints. To re-discover your very purpose for life, with this main player you need to call upon the Lord. We need to use prayer to bring that out from within which has been hidden by the closed hand and the sealed pocket.

To pray is to cry to the Lord

This word 'cry' was used when meeting with a friend and telling him the whole story, and listening, waiting for advice before proceeding.[7] It is from the witness box. The cry goes out for the next witness and we listen to what the whale has to say about Jonah. What have the crew to say? 'That hibernating creature, him who had a constant ministry of lying on his back, as we bent ours in the service of the ship.' Five times the word 'cry' appears in this book. Every time it is mentioned, something new happens. The hills as waves are rolled back, and we see pictures of the future forming in the waters. The same Hebrew word is translated 'seek' in Numbers 24:1, it suggests a coming nigh. Coming to where the cry can be heard. David said 'I called, and the Lord heard me'. He is describing the call of the young deer, and the response of its mother. When we are in deep distress, we are in the place where crying or calling can be heard. It is as the cry of the baby in peril to a mother. It sounds like the cry of a child or the bleating of a lamb.

Let all this lead us to that place of true repentance, where the sloth of sleep is flung on one side, and we take upon us the whole armour of God. Discovering what is covered in all our hearts. Whatever is talent to you, take it to God, as that rescued and precious.

Notes

		3	Acts 27:17	6	Acts 28:1
1	Hebrews 4:16	4	Jonah 1:5	7	Jonah 1:2,5,6,14.2:2.3:8
2	Jonah 1:6	5	Jonah 1:6		

CHAPTER 9

The description of your talent

The world around us will see what we are, and using that Yorkshire saying, 'calling a spade a spade.' They know what you are wearing under your jacket before you even take it off. If there is loose change in your pocket they have counted it before you have let it chink. Before this man with many aspects was called before the throne of God to give an account of his stewardship, he was called upon to give definitions to the captain of the vessel and the crew. The place around him became the whole theatre, and the world was listening, waiting with bated breath. He is placed, on awakening, within the circle of their fellowship, and they have quite a few questions to ask him which demand the correct answers of the English Teacher or the Accountant. At this point it is quite useless to develop an unholy stutter, to get around the questions asked. Jonah should have said 'I am what I am by the grace of God.'

We must give a reason for the hope within us

There are moments when we want straight answers to straight questions. What defines and determines what you have and are in Providence? You determine the ship by its shape, what it does, and where it operates. There is a need for more than a simple definition, but there is a requirement to touch the real nature of His calling. There must be the going to the flame of the fire, and feeling the heat as the ashes are turned over. When we tell our hearts, the truth the whole truth and nothing but the truth we have come to the real altar. Those who take shelter in truth will be hidden in truth.

We should not think of ourselves more highly than we should think.[1] We must think, and give an account of our gifts and callings as the Supreme Goodness has revealed them to us. Thankfully Jonah had not gone so deep into sleep, so that what God had called him to be, had been buried forever in the memory of that sleep. It wasn't locked in requiring some code for contact. It was not wasted or lost in the moment of the happening. It has not been jettisoned when the ship seemed to be sinking. The safest place on earth, at this time was where his talent was. Back to the Hand opening as some flower, and giving the scent as a gift. It hadn't been given as food for fish or as some play doll for mermaids. It was right where God had placed it, within his heart. There is that word sealed within him, given by the impressions received from the Lord.

Tell the truth about trials and triumphs

The world will always appreciate the real thing. They know the bad apple in the barrel even as these men of the oar suspected Jonah. That received from God needs to shine out. As these enquiring men held open the door, so the rarities of the man went through that door and he began to tell them the story of what had happened. Thankfully, at the end of a long story, there was a glorious conclusion.

The evidences of your ability are with you. They are not on some raft adrift or on some desert island. They need setting free for all to see and share. You remember when the New Testament missionary, Paul was on board the vessel, and they hadn't eaten for quite a while. He exhorted them to take some food, and as they were eating he makes a statement which was more than food. 'I believe God,'[2] not about God, not in God, but God. As it says on the coins of America 'In God we trust.' A man's gift will make room for him. The answers he gives go as snooker balls to the pockets. They sink deep, and make men think. They, immediately draw an inference from the interference, this man is a runaway from the Creator.

We are called upon to testify often

Here is a fish out of its net and depth. He suddenly stands out like a sore thumb, and they are all for emphasising that soreness. They do not offer a healing remedy, but they want to add injury to what has already happened to him. There is no plaster offered by the ship's doctor. There is no tarpaulin large enough to cover his failure and lack of faith.

The person of ability is fully armed. There is that clothing with comfort, which was given through the gifts by the Holy Ghost. He need fear no questioning, he need fear no foe, for foe with the help of a Friend can become a friend and not a fiend. He suddenly could have had more power than the captain or crew he is dealing with eternal things. There are things within us of a spiritual and eternal value, this world never knows or recognises. That man who has lately been robed in sleep, and robbed by that sleep needs to step out from under the cover. The great Jehovah Jireh will grant us that extra help when we are in a 'time of need.'[3] The calmest and the most holy place on this ship is where the man of desires stands to testify. Mark that place, and stand there yourself! Feel totally at one and at ease as you tell of what has been given, and the rough sea or passage has not managed to wash away or so mix it, that it appears mixed up without lines of demarcation.

The ability to testify is granted

It is a timely word He grants us. When we thought we were made speechless through sleep, we find our tongues have been re-born into saying what God requires of us. The tongue is loosed, the strings of it are touched, and it is ready to speak wrapped in words most precious. God is always ready to put descriptive words into our mouth to describe and define the tools of our trade. As salt is added to water to aid us in speaking freely, so suffering produces the best language of love.

In adversity, in the heat and the melting, we discover reserves in core essentials we never thought we possessed. We must possess talents, and not be possessed by them. The hand is for the gun, but the gun not for the hand. That promised by God, and sent with him had certainly, up to this point been hidden under a bushel.* I can be squeezed into something so small that even a fish would not make a good meal of it although angels love to hear it. The size of that bushel was great. It was the size of a ship and a cabin. What you are is what you produce where you are. It can be the answers to questions, it can be a song in the night. This testimony and what was uttered was different to the snores in the night. Whatever it is, that is God stepping in and creating another rung in the ladder, and that you have fallen off can be placed there again. The great thing about the disciples shaking the dust off their feet is that they could begin again.

The moment to testify is granted to us

Wherever the ship was at this time, it had reached a port. It had reached one destination and was about to go into another realm with

---

* Bushel: Matthew 5:15, it was a measuring basket with which they measured corn. Sometimes things like candles and lamps were hidden under them for convenience.

Jonah. The real cargo was to be seen in talents having been placed in another hold, in his heart, but not revealed. Trying to hide what has been given is like trying to place your hand over the light of the day and limit it. 'Let every creature rise and bring peculiar honours to their king.' That peculiar is what you have, what you have in reserve. No other could do it. You accomplished it because of the way you are constructed. No one else could have done it like you. That told in testimony is the tale of your life. It is woven in your own heart. It is not borrowed from a book but revealed through a heart speaking out. The New Covenant word used for 'witness' is the word 'martyr'* and there is a certain death involved about being bold.[4] The testimony of Martin Luther was 'Here I stand, I can do no other.' You might only be a door, but at least you can open to others to let them pass through into something you may never do. William Carey, the famous Victorian missionary to India, used to speak in mining terms when they were lowered down the shaft to bring up coal. 'If you hold the ropes, we will go over the edge.' Even a duck has a quack, and some fish are called golden, they so colour the water, that without them it would be so plain. Keep digging deep. Let the word of God dig deep, and you will have something to say about what God is saying to you.

We are often cowards of conscience

We are reluctant to tell or say we have certain identification marks. The flower called the Violet has a beautiful smell, but, alas, the smell doesn't last very long in the human nose. The reason for this is that there is also iodine in this plant, and it takes away your sense of smell. One breath and we have sweet perfume. The next breath and it has gone. There is such a substitute as that only being plastic that we smell. It is not the real thing. It is manufactured and not faith produced. If you would find out the real character or flower from the plastic, let the bees in, to work on them as King Solomon did! Plastic flowers produce no honey! How like Jonah this was! Always keep the freshness of your objectivity and experience in God. Solomon's Song says 'Our bed is green.'[5] It is a symbol of first love and the devoted, talented heart. God had

---

* Martyr refers to one who witnessed a good confession. That confession cost them their lives. Through dying they lost their blood; the word means to witness and to die as your blood is shed.

to throw water at him to bring him out of his fainting fits. As you faint, your dream falls with you. Everything about us can be turned to water. We become the opposite of water being turned into wine. What should have been wine becomes water, and it is not set before the people first, but it is set there all the time as water. The world requires some sweet taste, but all we offer in this state is the taste of salt and vinegar.

It is very difficult and confusing to speak of a solid foundation if you are on a moving ship. Have you noted, unlike this sent one of the Old Testament, the ship kept true to being a ship, wherever it went and whatever happened? The captain didn't suddenly abdicate and become a crewmember. It took the storm to part the sealed lips of this wayward sailor.

The world likes to listen to an interesting story

The world wants to know why you buried your deposit, when they were sinking and why didn't you cry for help? Peter 'beginning to sink' cried 'Lord, save me!'[6] We can refuse to grasp the outstretched hand when it is needed the most. Like this sleeper the hand that should help is tucked under our bodies while we sleep. They do not want a Christ with folded arms or broken hands. Why didn't you step in and help? There was that within you which might have helped so much. As a star for re-orientation, or a star as Browning says in one of his poems, 'to steer her bye.' Jesus is that Bright and Morning Star. The Greek mythological story says that the god of sleep, we hold so dear, created the poppy. It is not the opium influence we need to dull our pains. It is a rose and not a poppy, it is the Rose of Sharon those around us wish to see.

Jesus witnessed a good confession

Like Jesus Christ before Pontius Pilate, he began to witness a good confession. Jonah was a Hebrew of the Hebrews. The highest degree of spirituality was to be a Hebrew of the Hebrews. You were two things in one, and doubly dedicated. Sometimes, the best way to get the sails to work, and to bring things back into their allocated ministry is to break the lesser things. If you would see the sails billow with fresh wind, then forget about the port, and break the oars. Scribble over the mapped journey you have already travelled. Do what the Romans used to do. They used to smash the bridge they had crossed over. They also burned the boats they had used to get from the ship to the land. There was no turning back for any of them.

There are some things we can hold back

When he is questioned about his mission, it became a real mediation turning out to be a real meditation of misery. He doesn't say he was an Israelite. Only half the truth is no truth at all. The term 'Israelite' was a domestic term, used when in Israel. He tells them he is a Hebrew. If you are the best, be the best. The term Hebrew meant a 'crosser over'*. It has a glorious history of noble men who pioneered the word. If the best you have is silver, then be silver, but not brass or wood. Don't be like that King of Israel who put shields of brass to substitute those of gold.[7] This is a half measure and half the truth. This deceit runs in the blood. If only he would cross over at the moment from the side of comfort, from the side of the ship to the side of Christ. He needed to be on the opposite side that he went to sleep on, where Pilgrim was laid in Pilgrim's progress where the sun did arise.[8] Cross over from that selfish and shellfish nature. You need the cross, to cross over. There is a pathway created for others as you cross over. There are always those clinging on to your coat. The Septuagint[9] gives this answer as 'A Hebrew I.' These Hebrews had a whole epistle written to them in the New Testament. Like this relative Jonah, some of them were ready to deny their Lord. The writer tells them 'If any man draw back, my soul shall have no pleasure in him.'[10] Meaning, 'if any man draws back from the colours.' As he stands under the flag of freedom, so let him remain there. 1 Peter 3:15, we must 'be ready', to give an answer to those who ask us. Be ready, be fit, and ready to ride. In Joshua 8:4, it is to be ready, like a soldier, ready to fire on the foe. No soldier will deny his weapons or his country and king. Ready to be brave, ready to attack. For I am also ready. Even the ship would have a name scorched into its timbers, telling others, what it suggested, and its history.

Our excuses are poor testimonies

The sleeper, turned into a speaker, says I will explain to you what Goodness has given to me, and put within me. He wants me to be a light unto the Gentiles, but I consider that I haven't enough oil for my own

---

* From the Hebrew word 'Heber', "one who crosses over". It is found in 1 Chronicles 8:22.

lamp. He thought when he went to his destination; there wouldn't be enough in the heart of the Sender to supply all those people with repentance and grace. It is rather like that woman in the 1940's World War, who when she saw the bombs falling and the ruin, wondered if the Government would still have enough money to pay her pension! His theology is really mixed with seawater! He that shows the way to others lighting their path also lights his own path. I have limited God so much, the power He has, and the nature He unfolds, I don't want to share it with the Ninevites. If this dove was running his own business, he was ruining it. Here was bankruptcy in all its poverty and pleadings. That didn't lessen what he had received. You cannot judge the market by the size of the apples it sells, or simply the size of its stalls.

We are all asked questions which demand answers

Who are you? Where are you from? Where are you going? A Hebrew, is that all? What do you mean? That alone is a gift from God. Abraham the Master of the Faith was first called that. You are but a dim flicker of him. All you have is the lamp, but not the flame you don't even have the wick. Abraham climbed mountains when he sacrificed. He didn't run away from it - he ran to it. That testimony had been slept on also. He came before them like some hibernating animal trying to tell of the winter that had just passed. He speaks as the man who has fallen overboard seeks to explain why it happened. The senseless explanation, which we seek to offer as an excuse for not using our abilities which is nonsense.

That so straight and true can be bent crooked. When we are, then there is that sacrificing Abraham, and not Isaac. We do that when we compromise our principles, and have no faith. Then Isaac offers Abraham on the altar. That language Jonah speaks, sleepy though it is, so sleepy, he might have found his fulfilment playing the part of 'Sleepy' in Snow White and the Seven Dwarfs. What he has obtained as gift from God. Give a reason for being here. Justify the space you occupy. A tree is a tree, a horse is a horse, a ship is a ship, but what are you? There must be an answer to what we are and what we have in God. If your gift is musical, then play. If it is vocal, then speak or sing. If it is your fingers, then show your dexterity. If you feel it has been turned, churned into water, then flow like water, and carry ships to their destination. Humpty-

Dumpty would have been all right. He was so good at balancing until he fell off the wall. The king's men could march so well, but according to the Grand Old Duke of York, there were times like us, when they were neither up nor down. Be as ivory as the piano note or better still, the elephant tusk. If you feel so small that you are only a fly, then fly!

We must use what we have

When the bells sounded and the seas roared, dear one, you never prayed. You never took your gifting, and used it as some oar. It is so easy to be a good one in the package. A piece of driftwood or the wooden spoon that they stirred Hebrew porridge with had more answers and information to render. He wasn't what he had been and he wasn't what he was going to be. The violin in the case, nobody really knows its skill until it had the bow moved across its strings. There has to be a rubbing or chaffing. Leave the end product with the Maestro. Oh, that the sunshine within might expand to the size of the sun! If only the twinkle in the eye of the one called and sent might develop into that as the stars above.

Talents buried are talents unused

With the bow unstrung the target is never struck. While we play hide and seek, there is always the possibility of hiding what Jireh has revealed to us. As the Chinese proverbs aptly states 'The journey of a thousand miles begins with a step.' He has so much enabling, but going nowhere, he becomes nobody and nothing. He loses his sense of identity. Lost like a particle of salt in the very sea around him. He might as well have been a potato in a sack. He lacked distinction, action and unction. Those creatures in the sea never seen or heard of have far more recognition than he is prepared to give, to what the Almighty has granted. As they were enquiring it was like the unwrapping of a Christmas present. It had been all covered up. Would there be anything worth having within it? Was he worth all this trouble? God thought he was, and the One you trust thinks you are.

What is our trade? To run until we are exhausted and then to go to sleep? That is a strange trade for anyone, to trade in grunts and snores. He was a prophet of the Most High. He could have had such an insight, and told them where they were, and what Adonai expected. He could have said 'Whose I am and whom I serve.'[11] Whose I am, I will serve. My business and yours is to serve the Living One, and live for Him, using all the weapons of our warfare. There should be no skeletons in the cupboard. No top drawer to put things into. What flame is to fire, I must be to God, and what water is to fish, God is to me. We all have a word from God about our work for God. Sadly, the sun sets, and the clouds appear, and we forget the beauty and majesty of the day when God spoke to us calling us into a work for himself. Come and work for me? No, come and work in my vineyard? No, come and work with me, let us go together. From this togetherness that acumen appears.

We occupy positions we were never called into

How many try to pass the time by filling positions they were never meant to fill! He wasn't called to sleep. He wasn't called to be a sailor or a swimmer, not even a fisherman. He was called to the fiery prophet's office. You can soon be a round peg in a larger hole than you were made to fit into. You can be a square peg with no hole!

This story is connected with Matthew 25, and the Parable of the Talents. As we mentioned earlier, the word 'talent' means that which balances. When I would be pulled down or to one side, it pulls me back onto an even keel. It will act as a balance all your life. The ship had ballast. That granted by Providence is to keep you on an even keel. We are perfectly happy, and well balanced when the turn of skill is fully operating. The world is the operating room. Accent will tell your place of birth. The things we like or don't like will tell what we love. It was said of Peter 'Your speech betrays you.'[12] The thing we use will tell our usefulness to Elohim. If He is going to craft lives, He requires a model.

We are called back to the beginning

They asked him 'Where do you come from?' This immediately took Jonah back to the beginning. It meant he could make a fresh start from the beginning. If you would commence again, then go back to the beginning. If you would find what you have lost, then, go to the place where it fell. Let ability sail its own boat. Let your fingers do the talking. Let them do the writing. Let your forte do the talking. Let your zeal for God burn.

Ninety percent of genius is hard work. The rest is more work. The old English proverb says 'Some are born great, some are made great, but some have greatness thrust upon them.' Working with your armour does not mean you have to be in a large place. All taking place in the life of this deserter took place on a small boat. It is in a small theatre that great actors are born. It is the small theatre that the English language is learned and you are crafted how to use it. How did the world's great footballers learn their trade? How did they develop their talents? Some of them by kicking a football, endlessly against a brick wall. It didn't do a lot of good to the football or the wall, but it developed their talented feet.

We can lose sight of our leader

We can lose sight of the One, revealed in many functions who is leading us. A lorry driver in Hull, North Yorkshire, England was driving in one of the 'pea soup fogs' that used to be a speciality in the nineteen fifties. He asked his mate to get out and lead the way. This he did. After a while the fog seemed to lift, so Fred said to his mate, leading him on, 'Get back in now, George, the fog seems to have lifted, and I can see my way through.' The man leading the lorry answered, 'My name isn't George, I am out for an evening stroll.' He had lost the one who was leading him. As you travel life's pathway, being used and using what has been granted, be sure to close the gates and doors behind you. Then, nothing will trouble you from the past, if the door is closed, the hand of the past cannot reach through it, and drag you back. Let the ships of torment and bad memories stay in port. If they sink let them stay at the bottom.

Some people are self-made, and they worship their creator. Others think they are so endowed, they give gifts to God. Some are man-made, and they worship those around them. Some are God-made, and they worship that creation in participation of whatever He requires. Whatever He gives, they take it and use it for the glory of Emmanuel. God uses the wind and the storm to tune the instrument. There is an old Yorkshire saying 'Give a Yorkshire-man a halter, and he will soon find a horse.' He will build on and add to whatever He receives. Feel about your endearments what the Giver feels about them when He speaks in glowing terms. Golda Meir, one of the Prime Ministers of Israel said 'We always have the advantage over our enemies, because on this earth we have no where to go.' Let our escapes and escapades all enrich us as they are found and founded in God. There is more to follow from the hand of God and his heart which has already given us so much. Let us tell people we are the 'companions of God.' That is 'one who eats out of the same pansion* or dish.' We are those who eat from the same dish. Our food is His will. If there are any bones which stick in the throat, that is when we have tried to interfere in the cooking of the food in the fellowship. We are here; not to please ourselves, but to please Him, by being fully used for Him who sent us. He who sent you takes you, sometimes sleeping, sometimes kicking and screaming with every nerve of reluctance working against Him. He fashions you, and takes you to where you can be used the most. Everything that happens is to make us greater, easier and noble.

That given to you is being shaped as it is shared

The talented knight is one fully armed, who has gained his spurs, and he is riding back into battle after winning the one before. That given to you is being shaped, sometimes by shame and hurt, into a crown. Life's hurts are to form the gems in it. In the centre of it will be the 'Pearl of Great Price.' If you are only a boat, God has a fishing expedition for you. He wants you to carry Jesus around the world. Whatever you are, and whatever you see yourself as, be a good one. Be one that everybody else would like to be. Let your grace be like the sword of Goliath, for the king said 'Give it to me, for there is none like that!'[13] The person using all they have for God is rarely bored. Jonah stands to tell, but doesn't stay to go back the way he came from God.

---

*   The pansion was used for mixing the bread mixture to make dough. From here it was placed in the oven after being left to let the yeast rise. Fruit and other good things were often hidden in it. 'Companion' is from two Latin words 'com' and 'panis' meaning bread. A person who shares your bread.

Notes

1	Romans 12:3	8	Pilgrim's Progress written by John Bunyan while in prison
2	Acts 27:25		
3	Hebrews 4:16		
4	Acts 4:31	9	The Jewish translation of the Old Testament into Greek
5	Song of Solomon 1:16		
6	Matthew 14:30		
7	1 Kings 14:26,27	10	Hebrews 10:38
		11	Acts 27:23
		12	Mark 14:70
		13	1 Samuel 21:9,10

CHAPTER 10

The talent is concealed in many ways and realms

We carry a mistaken conviction that if we run long enough and quick enough, we can out-run the living God. You can run until your legs disappear into the ground. If you travel the circle He is always in the circle. If you journey oblong or square you will meet with your Maker around each corner. You are dealing with One who has the ability to create wings and fly further than you can ever run. Legs were the products of His life. Like Jonah, we think as long as we have paid the fare, justifying what we are doing, then all will be all right. We can sail from any port, and all the sea will be the same. This is a mistaken realisation. The stretch of God is larger than the whole history of man. When we are only beginning, that which we run away from is travelling back, with what we intend to bury even before we have discarded it!

God has many ways of bringing us back

Admitted, God brings it back to us in a different form many times. It might be wind, waves or a whale, but the Great designer will complete and compliment the work He has for us. That concealed becomes congealed. He that was with us at the beginning is waiting for us at the end of the matter, and He makes it appear as if it is only the beginning. As we run away, He runs towards us to arrive at the point we are going to even before we have commenced the activity. I see the reflection of Him in the man waiting to greet me. Everything I am accosted by holds some reflection of Divine activity. It isn't always within the soul. The hand of God comes in different shapes and sizes but all the shapes and sizes fit me. There was such an appearance to those travelling along the Emmaus Road, as He appeared in another 'form'.[1] Hebrews 1:1 speaks of 'fragmentary portions.' He takes all the mistakes out of my failings. That thrown away reappears in the form of a kiss or something just as beautiful. Count nothing out, but all in when you have dealings with this Sovereign.

We sometimes have to preach to ourselves

Jonah in his description of Jehovah is preaching to his own heart, but that heart is not responding. The Bible advice is 'physician heal yourself!'[2] The best ointments of life are those that have been tried as 'home remedies' applied to local sores. The planks of the ship may creak as the sea is spilled over them, but from the heart of the hard one, there is no response. He is communicating truth of the highest order. Where I stop, God is there in that realm. When I hesitate, as the Master, He shoves me on. Where I hide, He is hiding there not simply to hide but to share. What I bury, I bury in Jesus to be raised from the dead. In God, things are deathless. They keep re-appearing like the head of the cow through the hedge further down the road. What I refuse becomes that planted by the Lord. Did someone toss that thorn bush out of their garden that they used for making the crown of thorns? That man who said 'Why does this cumber the ground?' Was that tree taken and the boat, pulpit and cross that Jesus used made out of it? How many have gone to 'Car Boot Sales', and have seen the very things they threw out on a stall for sale at a very great cost. We have lost use for them. As far as we were concerned they had lost their usefulness.

Broken pottery can become Best China

Harold Degbie, a Salvation Army officer wrote a book called 'Broken Earthenware', and in it he tells of rescued talents, made whole by the pleadings and breathings of God. A shawl of pretence never covers the Giver or the gift. What we think is a cover becomes a veil to hide His presence when He is dealing with us. Starting with His peace, God pieces us together. The pattern has been formed as we have passed through the storm. The broken bits are not glued but formed with fragrance. There is something so beautiful about his handy work.

God is waiting to be discovered in every realm

He begins, when the spotlight is placed upon him by telling his congregation what God is and illustrating what God is not. There is no sphere where God isn't found. Here, (Jonah 1:9) he mentions the areas that were known to the Hebrews. He is all God in every place. God is the open hand and the open book. He is as open as the captain's map spread out on the table for all to see where they are. The preacher is saying 'all things are open' before God. He is not some idol, having eyes and seeing not, having hands, but unable to feel or touch. God sees all and knows all because He is all in every place. Wherever Jonah goes, He has been there. The fingerprints and footprints of God are everywhere. Many a person has removed a shrub or bulb from the garden and thrown it away, to see it win the prize at the local flower show. This Saviour with His eyes closed sees more than we do with ours open. Our vision is limited to here and now, but Elohim sees near and afar off. He takes a look into the future. His eyes go through the separating veil between day and night, year and eternity.

It is so useful to hear a testimony, but what if it is to our own hearts? The challenge is to realise that our theology must become truth in aprons and shoes. We all need a slice of the Bread of Life to sustain us. God is placed on the pinnacle that He deserves. If only that hidden in gifts could be placed where it could be used?

The greatness of God must be measured and seen in us

There is a hollow ring about his preaching. It is so hollow it is empty. We can all tell of the greatness of the Lord God. That greatness must be measured in us, as it should have been measured in the messenger. We can make Him the Lord of every area, but the area of our forte. In that sea there can be a little Island that I am the king of. He can be the One who does so much in other lands, in earth, sky or sea, but my heart is untouched. He calls God by name, but the best names given to this Deity is that born out of experience and intimacy with Him. In the early chapters of the Bible, God isn't revealed in all His names at once, but name by name is added until we have the whole pattern and picture.[3] The epithets given to this Lofty One in Jonah 1:9, should be a reflection of what He is in our lives. Matthew 5:48, where we are told to 'be perfect as your heavenly father is perfect' meaning to have all parts working. It is to have acumen fully working. Have all your journeying in full operation for your Maker. That given and distributed by God is as big as anything you will ever require. This is too large to hide in land, sea or heaven. There it will be known as it is known. It will be shown for what it is. We will realise what accomplishments were within our grasp.

There will always be capacity for growth

That as small as a straw could have grown into a ship. It was God who gave the instructions to Noah for the building of the ark. The same God gave the directions for the building of the tabernacle and the temple in Jerusalem. All these objects were made out of small substances, but because God was involved they became great in usefulness. Each became the wonder of their day.

Jonah calls Him 'the God who made'.[4] Immediately there is the suggestion of the spice of life and the abundance of variety. There is abundance in variety. The God, who is making, has made and will make. He keeps turning it inside out and outside in until it is what He wants it to be. He is doing it as the missionary speaks, shaking the sea like a blanket being shaken to remake the bed and to lend to it a new form.

God can arrive in all shapes and sizes

God turns up in some strange places. He comes, shortly clothed in a great fish. The 'God who makes' is making me, to bury the tools He uses is not part of the plan. All happening need never have happened. They were not part of the plan, they were brought in as extra soldiers. We all must pass through what John Bunyan calls 'The land of Forgetfulness' which was so green and pleasant.[5] You cannot take God from the Bible, and just learn of Him through reading or seeing. It is more than seeing the Eternal in action. It is fulfilling His call, and in that there is the discovery of who God is.

Lordship leads to true maturity in manhood

As Jonah speaks it is the first of twelve times that the word Lord is found in this book. The Covenant God that he could not keep covenant with. Fish will stay in the sea. Even a small coin can be held safely in the palm of the hand as a ring can be kept on the little finger during a storm. The smaller creatures will all make the sea their home but not this man and his God. God has to be made Lord of every chapter, word and line. God is where we are. This Deity does not seesaw on our moods. He restores and seeks to restore to the prophet what moth and rust does not corrupt, which is eternal in the heavens.

He operates in different dimensions

We are in one sphere made up of length, breadth, height, and depth. There are no corners for Him to peer around in a fog. God is in these and all other realms that we know not of. We can't enter into the moods or feelings of another, but He can and does. Bury your enabling, turn deaf ears to His voice, and you make the God of unlimited power, the god of limited power. Our ways and attitudes put fences around the Creator. We limit Him to bless the heart that beats. We can and do close the gate on His character. We sometimes spill the whole bottle of ink over the plans, and they appear as a blotchy mess. God re-writes them with the same finger with which He wrote the Ten Commandments and the hand that sent quails and manna to a wandering people.[6] In all the areas he mentions where God rules, he forgets that the Greatest of All is not in sky, earth or sea, but in the human heart. When we bury what He has given we bury the very throne He should be seated upon and rule from. If He is not Lord here, He is not Lord anywhere. The word 'king' in the English Language comes from a root word which means 'one of a kind'. A chief or leader. It also means 'he who is capable.' The one who is able. We know who that One is.

He limited God to his theology

The Hebrews believed that God was only in their country. That is why it is written 'He went out from the presence of the Lord.'[7] Jonah had the mistaken notion; that if you travelled out of the country the Creator would neither see you or follow you. His Master needed to grow so much larger. He has the whole of the world in His hands, but He leaves a place for Jonah and us.

The one who is served is not only the God of heaven but of earth and sky with the sea thrown in as some additional expansion. You can discover the greatness of goodness in all these areas. You must discover that magnitude is right where you are. Underneath and above that hidden is the very hand of the Infinite. Where we stop we limit. What is left behind in hiding, is never hidden from the God that sees me.

God is never absent or missing

He is the Principal of the dry land. The very land we travel together with Him. He is never absent from it. Jonah, how silly! He thought if he took a ship, he would leave God stranded at the harbour. He would leave God waving good bye. If he could manage to do that it would be the white handkerchief of the coward that he would wave. You must let His Majesty prove Himself in all wonders and areas. Tell me an area where God isn't, and I will tell you where God is. The atheist wrote on the little girl's piece of paper brought home from church, 'God is nowhere.' The little beam of sunshine read it 'God is now here.' You can't put God into areas as Jonah did, and think you have framed him in some picture frame. If you do He will step out, and stand right beside you. If you think God hasn't seen and doesn't know, He will beckon to you with His eyes and whisper deep things into your hearts avenues, the ears. That very area we say He is not, He appears. This Supreme Goodness came to the sea? No, He was in the sea before Jonah had paid his fare. We struggle to escape from where no escape is possible. God is a sealed area. 'None shall pluck you from my hand.' Ants in the Sahara desert find their way back to their holes by using the rays of the sun. God never leaves us without a light, leading us back to Himself. Don't leave the Master of this world for another world. Don't leave the God of the sea with its many waves for that so harmful and hurtful.

Jonah is saying one thing, but God is meaning another. Don't place boundaries around God. If you do, His hand will reach over and rescue that which you have enclosed. Stay with the horse bit and the bridle until the race is won. Stay with the ship in the storm until Providence brings it to dry land. A mistake had been made, but this Almighty loves rectifying small mistakes in a big way.

We must serve Him daily

The dry land represents the monotony of every day living. It is there where we tend to loosen the strings, and what we consider a burden, that God considers a gift falls to the ground. It is here we slip and slide, but He is the overseer of this. This dry land march suggests discipleship. More fail here than those who climb great mountains or achieve great things. We falter and fail the most on home territory, and among the things we are most familiar with. The late David Watson said 'If every Christian in the West was a true disciple we should have a revolution in our Christianity.'[8] The worst thing about the Christian Life is that it is daily. Daily faith, daily bread. The bleakness and the bareness of the dry land would give us the thin and the lean kind if it were not for the multiplying Hand. Although Joseph gave to Pharaoh the meaning of his dream, it was bareness and famine; he did not bury his talents.[9] He didn't become a husk or a withered plant. That very challenge was the means of promoting all that he was and had in his Redeemer from the pit. Pearls and other gems come from dark places. When Omnipotence draws you from them you bring a few rarities with you.

We must leave all to follow Him

We have to leave all and follow Him. He is that All that we require. Aesop tells the fable of how the snail received its shell. All the worms were called to a feast, but one worm so loved its home it wouldn't come. When questioned why it didn't come it replied that it was so comfortable it didn't want to come. Jupiter commanded that it should forever carry its house upon its back. What it might have been it never was.

When Jesus arose from the dead, He brought with Him gifts for men.[10] Gifts buried since the days of Adam. Gifts long forgotten. Whatever had been buried in the large, long hand of history was released in Jesus's resurrection.

God works in the thorn until it becomes a rose

God always works at the thorn until it grows a rose. The clay the Potter manages until the opals are found in it. If they are not it is fashioned into a beautiful token of the ability of the Potter. There is potential deep within us requesting to be brought forth. Spring snaps its sunny fingers and a thousand buds form. Even then it hasn't finished with them. They must be turned into leaves and then comes blossom, and the best, the fruit comes last of all. It all has to pass through the seasons. In each flower and fruit there is part of the cold as the finger of frost touches it. The wet and dull, the sunny and the howling wind have all left their moulding marks.

The titles, under which God appears through the lips of the speaker, leave the sailors in no doubt at all, that he is the cause of all the trouble.[11] He is the ship off course. There is something within him that is being withheld from his Deity. He has something belonging to Omnipotence, and that Master of the universe means to have it back where it belongs.

In looking for that covered, He looks for in the son of a man. Ephesians 1:10, found in the words 'gathered together,' the writer makes Jesus the Steward of the Ages.

When the hand of Providence digs it digs very deep

When the hand of the Supreme digs deep it digs very deep. It touches the slumbering chords of the heart again as the wind blows freely over the broken strings. They were in that present predicament through the doings or hiding of the man on board who stood before them. It only takes one word, and that becomes the initial evidence of all our troubles. All the activity, the foaming sea and the tearing wind was the activity of that named by Jonah. This was none other than the hand of the Infinite at work. What could hardened sailors and oarsmen do in comparison to Him? He swims while they sink. It seems as if God is going to take the landlubber down into the depths with Him. They don't intend to be partaker of this man's evil. If the wound is going to be placed in the salt, then let the man with the injury carry it there. God wanted to take the messenger through all these realms, so that he might discover the Creator and Sustainer of those realms. He would have come through them all, still intact, still wanting to serve and shine. Take another look at the story.

The throne of God is where you are

The waters are throne-shaped. In the book of Revelation His voice is the sound of many waters.[12] The waves are the chariots of good and gold. The winds are angels wings, sent to carry him to a place of usefulness and fruitfulness. The very winds can shape the shell that the pearl resides in.

If you would have a fresh breath of the Living one, then take a breath of this wind. If your salt has lost its savour, then come with me to these waters. If you are in the doldrums, come and sail on this sea. What a challenge awaits all that dare, for those who dare do! The very waves would dip in as the hands of Deity reaching out to catch that fallen from us. There needs to be a raising of the dedication to the task. If we hide in some lofty spirituality or spiritual happening, Omnipotence is there. Hide with the sailor, the farmer the aeroplane pilot, God is there. The Creator of heaven presents streets of gold and pearly gates, singing angels and songs, which never fade away. When we are dedicated to the task God has given to us, that means heaven on earth for us. All that accomplished is the Kingdom of Heaven on earth. The Lord's Prayer is answered 'Let your will be done on earth as it is in heaven. Let your Kingdom come.' You can have all the three realms in Infinity of heaven, earth and sea. That being used by the King of Heaven is heavenly. It is His Kingdom coming on earth. Not a little established here, there, everywhere and nowhere, but that done deep in the heart. God can deal with the human heart, and then He can deal with the world. He doesn't work it all out in the worlds and planets, then come to earth. He commences here where Jonah is.

There is a place for one and all

As in the sky there is room for every star, sun and moon, clouds and flying objects, so there is room in God's province and providence for your life. Let your life express His life in every realm, then those who have gone before, and those who have to come will rise up from small to great and call you blessed of God.

Do not make Him the Supreme One of earth and sea, acknowledging Him as the Supreme One in heaven. He hasn't only three points to His crown. His power here is but small compared with the magnitude of what shall be. Heaven where every talent shall sing its solo to the God it acknowledges. He is the Master of body, soul and spirit. He must conquer in all of these provinces. The Kingdom of Jesus Christ shall be delivered unto God.[13] From one far reaching realm to another with Emmanuel on your side and at your side. Nothing will be hidden, buried or run away from, because you can do all things in all realms through Him. Take that statement and baptise it in the swirling waters around you.

Notes

1   Luke 24:13-35
2   Luke 4:23
3   See Genesis and Exodus.
    The different names given
    to Abraham and Moses
4   Jonah 1:9
5   Pilgrim's Progress by John
    Bunyan

6   Exodus 20:1-7.
    Deuteronomy 8:3
7   Jonah 1:3
8   A Church of England
    Minister who worked in
    York, England
9   Genesis 41:7-32
10 Ephesians 4:10-12

11 Jonah 1:9
12 Revelation 1:15
13 1 Corinthians 15:24.
    Revelation 11:15

CHAPTER 11

The refusal to have your talent reinstated

The more God speaks, the harder we row against what Sovereignty has declared shall be. When the storm had reached full force, instead of them giving in, they dug in their oars, and tried to dig their way to land[1]. What has been written in stone and cast in bronze we seek to print in water to be washed away or brought in and out with the tide? They knew why this had happened from the lips of the man who testified. The net is thrown around them, and it is impossible to escape, but the sailors and Jonah know a thing or two about the sea.

We try many methods to make it on our own

There are other methods to be tried. When there is no escape from the Hand, we use the worst possible means to get free, but in doing so we find greater bondage. When the sails were torn apart by the strong winds and waves, they began to pull on the oars to accomplish their desires. They would be found wanting in their ability to resolve this situation. The crew think they can make it on their own. To do this you must paddle your own canoe after creating it. How wrong they are! They didn't travel very far before realising that it takes far more than an oar and a few strokes to defeat God. All cunning does not outwit or out manoeuvre the workings of the Lord. You can try to overcome a river with a thimble, and that teeming down a waterfall, trying to use your shoe to empty it. What God has said cannot be rowed or towed away. It is never sunk and never wrecked. The sea surrounding them was as great closing jaws, ready to crush the very life out of them.

We all lean heavily on the oars, and s how such dedication when we are trying to accomplish things for our own purposes. When they were added together with the help of friends, when they were multiplied from one to many, the many didn't add up to any great accomplishment. They were as straws floating on top of the water.

Sometimes we are just going nowhere

Swirling around but building nothing and going nowhere. All together, working against God we couldn't move a matchstick let alone a ship. Props are kept ready to lean upon if all else fails. They are kept in reserve to try to make the unreal seem real. All is a waste of space and effort. They went neither backwards or forwards, rather upwards and downwards like the waves they were trying to control. The real reason for their plight was the idol on board, cast in the shape of rebellion. The idol on board the ship was Jonah. He was worshipping himself. All the plans and wishes were not ready to be smashed. All that kept back, deposited by God in a human heart was not ready to be surrendered. We can take one thing and use it in the place of another, but that doesn't make it more acceptable. The oars must be dealt with. Even these can be broken by the waves. It is in the human heart where the battle of swirling waters and dangerous rocks is taking place. We all have oars, as part of our own self will. We all recognise the colloquial saying 'putting your oar in.' Through them we are ready to demonstrate our independence, waving the oar at the storm as we row.

Here is the story and history of the human heart

This story is the story of the human heart. Here we have the finest art form depicting it for us, but it more than art form, which can be lifeless. This is dramatic theatre, being acted out before the eyes of the reader Here is but one heart and life in Jonah from it. There are abilities within all of us to resist God even down to an oar. We sometimes give Him the larger things, but resist with the smaller, and we don't think they count. What we do is an indication of what we are. The oar must take on the shape of the Cross of Christ. This is your way out of the rough passage, as you fling yourself on the cross you float through.

The mercy and callings of God are unlimited. No shepherd ever called his sheep as often and as kindly as God calls those who have laid aside their destiny and testimony. He wants to bring them home rejoicing, but without the oar of their own self efforts. Elohim uses His hands to rescue us, not wooden oars. Sealed orders had been delivered to the man about to be marooned on some island so deserted, that even the sun doesn't shine on it. All that potential in Jonah is reduced to an oar, but not the love of God. As those things become narrower and smaller in the shape of an oar, the love of God grows bigger and better by the blade. The Love of God is larger than the heart of one man. All the hearts and human needs are met through this Lover of men. It is deeper, wider and fuller than any sea. As they dip their oars, if they dip them deep enough, the Hand of help will be found around them, and underneath the ship.

We resist the call to return as we resist change

We will not return in repentance. Every oar pulled whispers the same message to the sea. You can cover an oar with water but it still remains a wooden oar. Call it by any other name; it is still refusing to give to God what He has given to us. There is no growth in an oar. You cannot plant it or read from it. Oar it is and so it will ever be. It is found here as a figure of self will. When we are of this disposition, our usefulness and talents can be measured by the water which is left on the blade as the oar comes out of the water. If only we could hide as the wooden peg did when it was placed in the water. He wants that from you with 'usury' - with interest. The very word 'incentive' suggests keeping to the tune. If God is playing it, then I must be singing it, not as some bawdy sailors' ditty, but as the Song of the Soul set free. If Redemption is the song then let me be the chorus. You can plunge, pull and row, but it doesn't alter the heart of the one who has taken that given and is seeking to run away with it as that stolen by a thief. How can you hide that which cannot be hidden?

The first step is the worst step

The first step to the throne is the worst step and the steepest when a man returns to his Maker. Once we have taken one step. It might only be an oar's length, but God will take so many steps towards us. More steps than the waves of the sea. More steps than there are granules of salt in the sea. This is not seaweed love which is swept away to be cast forgotten on some remote beach to be bleached by the sun into powdered fragments, and if not found tangled and withered. God's desire is to get to the heart of the matter and deal with the matter of the heart. His overtures are many. He has composed love serenades, more words and tunes, set to the music of the seas to ask us to take up the challenge afresh. Here is 'water music' in full recital and volume! All coming from the sea is fresh. What the Challenger has asked of the prophet, is struck on the head with an oar. If it doesn't succeed the first time, it is beaten with many stripes. You cannot control the raging sea with a wooden peg such as this. There is no stopping the might of the Eternal. The smallness of our hearts beats it as with some oar, with some wooden fist. On the sixtieth occasion of beating will it submerge that seeking to arise to help us all? Take that oar, that self expression, that which you dig others with, and turn it into the first step back to God, as you surrender it.

We always try new methods of escape

They thought it would be good to try some new method. To try something they were at ease with, you know, the familiar things of life? They had called on their gods but to no avail, the storm had continued unabated. Their prayers had come to sit on the ship rails as birds of all weathers to mimic them as they called. They would turn to the familiar almost as familiar as Bible quotes to the one who reads it, but hiding the fact that they were not for giving in yet. Our circumstances and rough passage have a greater work to do before we surrender ship and oars, and all there is about us to God from where it came from. It must be the submitting of the oars to save the ship. The small decision makes way for the large thing in our lives. Give Him the handle, and then the blade will follow! The small pilot will bring the great ship into port, through rock and reef. The small rudder, placed in control of the owner will do its work if used rightly. If only I could fly as some bird to the nest, the crow's nest high up on the mast of the vessel, where land, treasure ships and floating drifters were sighted. What Sovereign power has tried to say to this man might as well have been a drifting boat with no cargo and no direction, simply going by and unheeded because of the notice this human being took of it. There is a way to escape in surrender to God. 'Imprison me within your arms, and I shall conqueror be.'

We can and do ignore the advice given

God speaking can become a piece of floating debris. These men trusted in sight, sound and taste. They trusted as natural beings in the familiar. They had used these paddles to success before. Things tried and tested rather than the Jehovah of Jonah. Try reading some book. Try coming to the problem from a different angle that may ease the stress and stretch of conscience. You can solve the problem by not being part of that problem. The timbers of the ship, as they were stretched in the storm said, 'repent,' 'give in,' go on.'

They had been told to throw Jonah overboard. Throw it into the lap of providence. The talent could have been re-committed, but they were not ready for that just yet. A little more difficulty and a few more creaks and groans, and they might be prepared. The Worker has to employ more skills before the worker is fully equipped, and able to take all the stress and strain. They had to be prepared for what the Great One desired for them. Doing what they should have done would have thrown Jonah immediately back on God. Put him into such deepness that he can't swim out of it, under it or through it. When we take the plunge willingly or unwillingly, knowingly or not knowing, we are plunged into something quite new, and it is much bigger than the size of the oar, a token of our rebellion against Him.

Rebellion needs to be washed away

All rebellion would be washed away, and ground into fine sand by this machine called the sea. In the commitment that used for rowing, our own way will be lost. The hand will be flung open wide as the heart, as we are thrown into what God has prepared. There is a deeper work required in the heart than that washed by the sea. The next tide may bring it back. Rather than surrender we row harder. We will serve you better, as you command and deserve, but there is only the oars breathed between obedience and rebellion. Burying that given or taking it and using it, embracing it as Jonah's wife might have done on his return. 'We will do more for you.' We hand obedience on the oar, in the smallness of our minds. 'We will attempt new things for you.' 'No, it is less I want.' It isn't the many works as the oar is dipped below the waves into the salty serum, but one act of repentance will make it right. They were working in such a frantic effort to bring the wooden pulpit to land. We should be taking up that which we should be taken up with. When we take to the oars, ifs and buts, we are only drawing in water. Don't take from God with something the size of an oar. Attempt great things for Him - expect great things from Him. We are trying to empty the ocean, trying to control that trouble with some paper handkerchief. We are trying to empty the water out with a wooden spoon. When we act like this the wooden spoon is all we get. It is all we win. Our accomplishments are seen in the size of this stick used for rowing. It becomes the rod for the fools back.

There are no lasting effects when we rebel

There is no lasting effect or evidence that we have been there with our little peg stirring the water area. As you look back over the sea, there is no evidence that you have been there, or that a ship has sailed by. To obey the Universal Lord is to write with a pen of iron in rock. All remember men who have done great things for God. There are those heroic people who have refused to rebel against God, and in doing so have refused to bury their talent. They have written their works on the pages of the hearts of mankind. If you don't want to write in water, but in a better and more lasting substance then try obeying God. It is the most secure place in time of wreck and ruin. Try saying 'yes' to His calling, and seeing through to the end, what He has destined you for. God has written His best works in the rich, red blood of the cross of Jesus Christ, a greater than Jonah, and Creator of the man of the oar. The soldier doesn't retire as the light dawns on another day and the reveille sounds. When the ship's bells are rung, there has to be the distinguishing between what the stormy sea does, and that which is deliberate and true. There are so many noises heard as we sail the seas, but one of them is a voice – the voice of God. There are some false words and calls, but we must respond to that under the captain's hand. The sounding of ten bells doesn't mean the end or the beginning of the voyage. It is only part of it. We must never make the partial the full. The fragment can never be the full loaf. We are still in charge until that causing the offence is thrown overboard as cabbage leaves, and as it plunges it makes a louder splash than an oar.

Don't try and help God out

Don't launch a boat of help to rescue that given back to its Creator. There is a total commitment as that is thrown into the sea. There are no half-hearted efforts, there are no measured methods, it is total. You do it when making your own plans. We are pulling on the oar against Providence, rowing against God-given principles when we refuse to have the talent reinstated. Once we find ourselves obeying rather than rowing, there are new ships of hope and desire to be launched from this very place. A Cross, to make it stand out so that we don't forget, marks it on the map of life. Anything for those serving the Master less than His complete will, is waste and bilge, and it must be tossed overboard while we are at sea. Those who refuse to hand back what has been taken, remind you of a warship coming out of a battle with scars as holes just above the 'plimsoll line', with funnels bent and deck blasted, rails missing and having an uneven lurch but still sailing. If you stand too close to take back what is being jettisoned, it will come back, blown by strong winds and strike you full in the face. Not a very pleasant experience! This incident proves we can return to God in word, spirit, conversation and manners but not in heart.

We can talk theology and spiritual as this reject did, but be as far away from God as this boat was from the land that it had sailed from. The King of these seas doesn't want part of you, He requires the real you. Not the packaging, but the content. Not empty shells, but those that have within rare content. He wants the real you then you can be really you.

There is real peace when we return to our Maker

As you return, the violent rush around you, the screeching sounds and the booming waters, can be a haven of rest, a rest of a peaceful place. There can be a sheltered island called 'The Will of God.' On the island of Samoa, the natives have built a roadway, and they named it after the conduct of their missionary. They called it 'The Pathway of the Loving Heart.' W. Shirley puts it in onyx fashion in the hymn 'Sweet the moments, rich in blessing.' 'Here it is I find my heaven while upon the Lamb I gaze. Love I much? I've much forgiven. I'm a miracle of grace'. Out of this rough sea, and into the river of His peace.

You can be a miracle, mirage or a mermaid. Two are fictional, one is fact and fixed. There was a time when no ship would carry such as Jonah. A Minister was not welcomed on board. Stories and happenings such has this did not help with the folklore that was woven around the religious types. He might interfere with their standard of living. Another flag might be hoisted called decency and holiness, and that would never be acceptable.

Talents are restored as we are brought back

In music, to repent* is to go back to the words. Go back to what is written. Go back to the Book! In the returning there will be the rotating

---

* "Repent" is printed on the music to instruct the singer to go back to the words

of the clay. That vessel will be turned upside down so that all the junk will fall out of it, and it can be put to its proper use. All the locks on the treasure chests will be broken open. They were hesitant to get rid of him, they might have to restore his fare. Their hands were held tight together. Just as this man of God was withholding that presented to him, to help him in his journeying for God, and leading a city into repentance? All that is wholesome about your personality is taken, sanctified and used.

We are always in danger of losing control

There is a humorous vein introduced into these wild happenings. The seriousness is sent up in a shower of foam from the sea. The hardness and the seriousness of the situation eased. They couldn't control the sinking barge, it was about to sink. They weren't in control of anything, so they took out their little oars as if to help the situation. You might as well hand a straw to a camel and let it break its back! It is almost as ludicrous as taking a penknife to cut a tree when the tree cutter had failed through lack of petrol. When the axe has faded into bluntness, using your finger or tongue to do the job. The sheep will not keep the sharp teeth of the wolf, lion or bear at bay by simply bleating. These people will not keep the ferocious sea at bay by simply rowing. Fancy trying to balance that against you on the end of an oar! Who can master the masterful with inadequate means? Rowing is not repenting. Effort is not always love.

Good works offer no evidence of a heart restored

The rowing is not the initial evidence of talent unearthed or brought from the depths of murky waters. Rowing is not repenting, it is not unifying, it is not ushering in the rule of God, and a new era of obedience. The weak sound of the oars doesn't sound the same as repenting. It doesn't sound like the bells on the bottom of the High Priest's garment as he went into the most holy place to offer blood for acceptance.[2] They could never offer water. The talent cannot be fished from the ocean bed with an oar. It is too weak, too short, too late. The wrong hand is wielding it. It might be influenced by another wood-shaped object called the Cross of Jesus Christ. That goes very deep, and reaches parts that other things cannot reach or touch.

We can hide behind things

There is much hiding behind 'oar ministry' as Adam hid with shame behind a tree.[3] There is such a doctrine of helping yourself. Paddling your own canoe when you place your own oar in, is still being preached by many a runaway and sailor. Substituting the little oar for the big Lord. Substituting the smaller thing for the larger thing called obedience can be the fashion of the day. The fashions of the day pass away. Substituting one for the other and not reinstating that ability to part of life, fragmented life.

The Septuagint version of the Bible says 'The men rowed hard to regain the land.'[4] As if there was a war on, and they needed to gain something that had been lost. This was piracy of the first order under the skull and cross-bone! It was regain to reign. There was some ground to be lost while they were at sea. In objecting to being used for God, there is that very thing which we long for, but can never have until we turn to return. It is the very ground that we bury our object of usefulness.

Do not challenge what you can never defeat

To take your stand for that you can never win, is suicide. To get more land and not the land that God has called you to be is to bury things deeper. 'The meek shall inherit the earth.' There is a certain quality of lamb nature, as we surrender. It is poor land indeed, and nothing will ever grow there for it is as the land of Sodom and Gomorrah. Even birds of paradise do not fly through it. It will only grow wild oats, but when they are harvested they will only be husks and the tares that Jesus warned us about. It might grow the food that the Prodigal Son would have eaten with the pigs in the far land.[5]

Dr John Gill, the Puritan commentator says of this rowing with the oars, 'They laboured with all their might as one digs a pit.'[6] Guess who was about to fall into it? They were digging a deeper pit for Jonah to bury himself and all his amenities in. They could have been digging to find the true gold buried. Away from God, our rarities hidden, we dig a bit deeper and create a greater hole. We find ourselves tangled in the mesh and mess of things around us. You can't really dig in water. You may dig, but the hole is as full ten days later as it was at the beginning. It is a labour in vain. For what you take out returns immediately, and all is as it ever was and shall be, hole without end. It is a grave without any bottom, a hell of their making, without the fire but wet.

You can push and shove and still not arrive

The word used for 'rowing' is used in other places of the Bible in Ezekiel 8:8, of breaking through or digging through a wall. The same Hebrew word is used in Job 24:16 and Amos 9:2, as if there was a hedge to be gone through or a door to open. Behind the door was all that buried away from God. Only God could open this door, and this rebellious one could help by becoming God's assistant in the school of obedience. It is a very strong Hebrew word used for 'row'. It means to push with all your strength. It suggests forcing a passage as if engaged in burglary. There will always be moth and rust stealing through to kill and destroy the birth of new adventures in God. It holds within its folds the thought of ploughing a field. This is not the field of his calling. If only we could be hidden in God as a plough blade in the soft earth.

There are some things that can't be forced

You cannot coerce God by beating Him with an oar. You cannot place God in such a small shaft of wood. Who wants to be buried on the back of an oar? In the water it was leading nowhere only to more of the same. When will we learn, when will we understand? Oh, to have a larger acceptance of what He requires than the size of a paddle. The wind cannot be kept at bay with wooden stakes. What they were doing, the strain and the sweat, it was simply going to take them to the place where they commenced. When they arrived they wouldn't know it because they would be right where they commenced. This is the frustration of the little oar. We do all the heaving, pushing and pulling but the idol remains intact. It is not even knocked off the shelf of the heart. It knows no unsteady stand. The challenge to give it up is reduced to the size of a stick. When we mix what the Supreme Being requires with what we want to do and our own plans, as this one did, then it is surely iron mixed with clay, and the image, however tall and strong at birth, cannot stand.

We just delay the inevitable happening

All this messenger was doing was delaying the hour and the day when God would have him leaning on Him for support. You can't get heaven or peace, not even a piece of heaven, not even direction or the assurance of the binnacle or compass out of a rod of wood. Even barnacles will cling to the bottom of the boat better than the deep congealing of Jonah's heart to his God. Giving to God, and giving that required by Him are taken and given from different accounts.

Any member of the Oxford or Cambridge boat crews will tell you the futility and the fatality of digging deep in choppy waters.[7] You cannot plough water, you can plough a field, but the sea cannot be ploughed. We can have lots of activity which means nothing but threshing the water. All our efforts can only be paddle and the tip of the oar deep. There was such activity but they were going nowhere, because God was at the helm and guiding the ship to the place he had prepared for it. What is achieved can be as the lifting of water on the blade of the oar. As water lifted out of the sea just to be placed back in again. Achievement can be the measure of an oar blade. Many times, we are just treading water with no real destination. That done can make a big splash but it can be as repetitive as an oar being lifted out of the water to be placed back in again. There was no real surrender of the heart of Jonah in all his activity. Self effort will never bring us to the centre of the large heart of God. When they could make no headway, they turned after much wasted sweat to getting rid of the idol containing the rare gems. They must get rid of that deeply seated and not surface top as these rowing bars were. They only pulled on the lengths of wood drawing self life in the water, using oars as pencils and pens, just as artists use them when drawing.

The idol must be despatched

They had to throw the idol overboard, and it might result in him taking up his enabling, and throwing away the crutch of his crippling. That would be taken up as the anchor is drawn up, and the ship is ready to sail away. Without that given he would be as a drifting ship without sail and no port that would recognise him, allowing him to come into land. Indeed, he would have been as Noah's ark without a rudder. The difference between this drama and that, is that God was on the inside of the one ark, and He closed the door from within, keeping people out.[8] Jonah had closed the door from within and was for keeping God out. Leaving Jonah on the outside not God, facing tempestuous times and swelling seas.

A four year old girl saved her family when the house caught fire by biting them as they lay asleep, unconscious of their danger. This is the sort of conviction we require to move us. A Minister was saved from a house fire in Manchester, England. Suddenly, at 2 am in the morning, the doorbell rang. He went to answer the door, and found no-one there. Then saw the smoke and the fire. No one could explain how it happened. That doorbell is your heart. Sensitive to His reach and touch. The latest invention for the humble doorbell is found in the fact that you don't ring it, you just speak to it. God has some wonderful ways of arousing us and preserving us. He uses many tools to elaborate and decorate His creations and awake them to their responsibilities.

Notes

1   Jonah 1:13
2   Exodus 28:33
3   Genesis 3:8
4   The Septuagint. The Greek Version of the Old Testament
5   Luke 15:16
6   Dr John Gill, the Puritan Commentator
7   Oxford and Cambridge are English Universities that conduct a boat race on the river Thames each year
8   Genesis 7:1

CHAPTER 12

The reason given why we bury our talent

The sailors did not ask God the simple question couched in profound terms so that any wanting to avoid it might treat it as a piece of floating debris. 'Why have you done this?'[1] It would always have been distant to anyone who was distant and hard of hearing. There were, and are, a mixed multitude of reasons why we cover up that richness of diversity. There was many an answer waiting to be called upon that day. Each one ready to fly its own flag from the country of his origin. They would provide both destiny and alibi for the feeling refugee. So many replies can be given, and so worded, as not to be the real reason. There are more reasons than reason can ever know, why we bury our talents. There was nothing here of 'beyond reasonable doubt'. There was no reasonable excuse. Our excuses sometimes become our crosses, and they are very heavy to bear.

We try to deny our involvement

Most prisoners of their crime deny any involvement. There are many facts in every faction seeking to turn it into fiction. When returned to God there are so many facets as that accounted as angled mirrors, turned into a diamond by the Creator and filled with light received while entombed. We answer most of the questions asked. We answer them by our action. Our deeds become our denials. The responses are in the clothes we wear and the attitudes we adopt as our own children. What we say is the pay we have received from such actions as the seer of God. He might have gone to sleep again, but replies were required. His voice and testimony must be louder and deeper than any sea.

The questions that doubts bring

Would he feel embarrassed? If the people he was sent to were not as heathen as he thought? Would the message of God be adequate enough to bring a response? Would his money be enough to see him through? Did he compare his deposit with that of those around him? Were they far more gifted in his eyes and heart? Here is an alphabet of questions and only the Alpha has all the answers. These like fish in a sea of despondency kept swimming around in his head. There had been others who had failed. His soul knew that right well. That given to him from the I AM, that commission was so poor when compared with others who were a great success. When we are guilty of burying our talent, we can adopt the rebellion of silence. Others, all that around him had something to say, but he had no song to sing. That dumb had struck Jonah. The problem for this man is the difficulty for all pioneers. No one had ever done this before as far as he knew. We can readily respond to God believing for a miracle when it has happened many times before. What about Noah and his work of building the first ark? We can look at other Prophets and New Testament figures that were so accomplished in God. We only look at the end of the matter, and not at the beginning where he was at this hour in God's timing.

There is a greater work to be done in the heart

The work is still going on, he hadn't arrived yet. The traveller hasn't even commenced his pilgrimage, he has gone the other way. There is still that which is misshaped as a coin with corners needing to be fully rounded. There is nothing as far from being square as that round, and nothing as far from being round as that square. He is spending the dull and dud side of a coin that minted in his mind. There he became a recluse. He carried in his heart more cargo than the ship. He was the recipient of a cargo of old rusty nails and iron filings. Most things that are buried degenerate into rust to be baptised in dust. As the ship would be with this sort of weight, the Plimsoll line was well below the water surface. Those false ideas about the character of God were as weighty as any anchor. With lead in his heart, he sinks below what is expected of the man of God.

There are so many reasons why we bury our talent

Did somebody say something to him when he began to demonstrate that talent? That said restricted his soul and turned friend into an enemy. When we place another tree to displace the Cross of Christ, it bears fruit, and these fruits are the reasons. We offer excuses; these are lies given other names. Was there a jealousy burning, shrivelling up his soul into the size of a grain of sand? The person who said the offensive thing, did they come from Nineveh? His stumbling block was a large as a city, the city of Nineveh.

I think one of the main reasons was he couldn't play 'second fiddle' to the Main Player. He was no puppet on a string. He had a mind of his own, and could rely on his own decisions. Could he? Did he think he was the only one? Every other one was a pebble while he was a pearl. It was such a shock when he discovered that God had other emissaries, while all he had was adversities.

God has many weapons for His warfare

There began a realisation how wrong he was, when his Master began to call up reserves. God had the whole of nature, as great as an army at His command. Every part of nature was willing to play its part from whale and worm to the waves of the sea. These were not men, or of the human kind, not even tools of brass or of iron but they were as wild as wind, large as the sea and as big as whales. When God begins to dig inside of us, big tools are used. Even the word of the Supreme is likened to a hammer, large sword and a raging fire. If he was in any doubt, God was going to use a worm. He uses both great and small, short and tall to help those with feet that run away with them. To help by directing them into the paths of peace. That was forgotten what we always forget. 'A Greater than Jonah is here.'[2] Our forgetfulness is lost in His forgiveness.

We look backward and upward but we forget to look inward

There will be times, times and half, a time when the Almighty will call us to give answers to serious questions. The speaking voice is seeking to unearth that hidden. We often look forward and backward but we forget to look inward. Every bad situation asks questions. They pose an enquiry. They are there as witnesses. They have sworn by the Bible 'to tell the truth, the whole truth and nothing but the truth.' We gaze at failure, and almost feed on the success of others, but we forget to look within, and find the answer to why we have placed beneath everything else what the Giver would place on top. We leave footprints in the Sand of Time for good or evil. It is sad that things go wrong because we are wrong. That very wrong becomes greater than the right. More excuses than notes on a piano, far greater than that deposited within. The excuses in his heart was greater in number than the sailors who sailed a great big ship. There are sacred and sure memories in all our hearts, some lodged there as honey, others as vinegar. We look to God to help us, but we forget that within which separates us from our God like a thick wall without doors or windows.

We have to be realistic in assessing ourselves

Take a look and see what he has achieved. There are no looming castles. He has travelled on no great journeys. The first brick has not been laid in the foundation. He is not pondering over the Architect's drawings. Even this journey never reaches its ultimate. There are no repentant sinners. He couldn't be used as he was because all his converts would be like him, and run away from responsibility. God never lets us sow our rebellion. Those things we accomplish ourselves are neither to be seen, heard, looked upon or cherished. There is such a thing as a bad dream in the daytime. That built by us in our covering up is just like a sandcastle, wind and rain destroying it. A wild fox will knock it over with its tail. The laugh of a mocker can unscrew it. Is it as the house which one of the three little pigs built that a wolf could blow down? Yes, here are the foundations for the 'House that Jack built.'

We all have memories pleasant and unpleasant

There are certain ships in the memory, which need a Man of War to sink. We provide or own seas for our ideas to swim in. That done by him was born out of fear and not faith. Fear will always strip you of your potential. Faith will build you up and add to it. All that is required in our work for God is bred and born within, and not put on as a flag on a rope, ready to be torn to shreds by the very thing, the wind that was meant to unfurl it for all to see the colour of its message. Jonah had to recognise that there was a little bit of another Israelite in his blood. The name of Rueben springs to mind, meaning 'that as unstable as water'.[3] You cannot run away from what you cannot escape from. Yet we try so hard. We think we are the train, and the tracks go on forever, dining in the buffet, forgetting about the buffer at the end of the line. The train can stop before the end of the line if it loses its driver or power. Memory lane runs right through the hearts better than a written history book. It should go from being history to being what the bible has to say. It should go from a lane to becoming part of the Way.

In burying one thing we bury many things

The salient factor here is not the burying of the talent but what he disposed of with it. In planting the tree we plant the roots as well. What did Jonah have within his grasp when he buried it. Think of the many things you buried with it? When the Pharaohs of Egyptian glory were buried, their talents, riches, silver, gold and all their service and servants were interned too. They placed more than flowers on a coffin. They had a forsaken and a forgotten history. The history of the spade is not so deep. There is so much sunshine hidden when we buried our heads in the clouds that surround us. We invite deep shadows on the sunniest of days. While our heads are under the water the best ships of all pass by. We miss so much while we are missing. Ask doubting Thomas?[4] We can and do dream dreams, but those in Joseph's bedroom are a reality.[5]

The real you is missing

While we are under the water as under the burden the real you isn't seen. While Jonah was asleep in the boat, under the water or in the whale, he wasn't seen. You only appear as half a person, even when you come to the surface for breath. When anything goes under the water to be hidden there is no memory or history of it written where it has been.

What is this you have done? Is an echo, a long sounding echo from the Garden of Eden? It sounds like a trumpet through the ages, a trumpet that has struck on one note. Mother Eve was asked the same question. What was asked of the procrastinator by the fellowship of sailors? The Septuagint version of the Bible puts it like this 'What, have you done this!'[6] All he had done was to turn a 'Midsummer's Nights Dream' into the 'Winter of Discontent'. James Joyce in one of his books puts the days of the week into some unusual language when we bury our ability. See if you can recognise any of them? Moanday, Tearsday, Wailsday, Thumsday, Frightday, Shatterday. There his days end, but I have added another for Sunday - Shunday. If you sow even one wild oat, left for a time, there will be such a multiplication.

We all need direction from the Throne

In the Old Covenant they had the Urim and the Thumin to tell them what to do, giving the nation direction from God.[7] A theological student asked an old cobbler if he knew the Hebrew meaning of them. He replied, "Why, I don't really know, but I know that if you alter two words you have 'usin and thumbing.' I have come to a ready understanding what the will of the Lord is simply by 'usin and thumbing". The Bible was his ever ready book, never closed but as open as the face of a plate.

A Scottish woman said she had devised a way to discern the will of God. She used to throw a stick up into the air, when she came to crossroads, and whichever direction the stick pointed when it landed, she went that way knowing that it was the will of Deity. One in the village decided to hide and watch her. She threw the stick up six times, and then proceeded to go in a certain direction. The person watching leaped from behind the hedge and asked her why she threw it up six times. 'Well, the way to the left is so much smoother than the other ways, and I kept throwing the stick up into the air until it pointed the way I wanted to go'. Having your own way will cloud every Fellowship you ever enter into. Wrangling as seaweed will be yours.

We are left with sand and charcoal

That left at your feet will be but sand and charcoal. He exchanges the mashing of the sea for the music of Nineveh. King Neptune replaced the king of Nineveh. They always played the flute when they repented in sackcloth and ashes. David Livingstone said 'I would rather be in the heart of Africa in the will of God than on the throne of England out of the will of God'.[8] Why be a Prime Minister when you can be a worker if you want to be, in God's will. In God's will, with your capacity being used up in many causes?

We arrive standing at the side not inside, but standing on the sideline instead of being on the playing field. The only thing our feet touch is tarmac, never squeezing a blade of grass under our tread. There is such a thing as spectator participation, and we are all so good at that. You don't have to be taught to watch, but you do have to be taught to play. We stand where no bruises are felt and no blood trickles down the face. There are no hard pressures here. We choose the quiet river rather than the open sea where salt smacks our faces. We are where no hurts are collected, but neither are medals received or knighthoods given. In that very place you find yourself hugging your golden glory, you never score

114

a goal. In 'touch', never dirty needing a shower, but as clean as a whistle and not blown. A mere spectator, but not a participator. No attention, no achievement. No involvement with any inspiration knows participation and knows inspiration. Buried to one thing and covered to most things. All that piled upon us when we are buried becomes too much to bear for we have less breathing space, and room for manoeuvre.

We are always ready to make our escape

Jonah was asleep for part of the time in the covered part of the ship. As near to the lifeboat as he could be without actually being in it. If they were going to sink, he would know nothing of it until the water filled his ears. Jonah had escaped into sleep and into another world of the dreamer. He made sure there was a ready access and way out if things went really wrong. This is why people run from place to place and from preacher to preacher. In the running and journeying we are just circling God. We arrive back where we were just short of breath. Feeling we have travelled everywhere but in the spiritual realm we have travelled nowhere. When we run we carry His crown with us, and we only stop running when it is placed back on his mantle.

He had gone to the sideline, but it is his side and not God's side. The Sovereign's side is that facing out to sea, towards the city he has been called to. How large was the gap between him and the Lord? As wide as the sea, and as far away as a ship has travelled from port in a couple of days. There seems to be more hope of sighting a Mermaid combing her hair in a shell mirror than this stray returning to the fold. This one had not just slipped away as a drifting vessel. What he did was deliberate. Jonah 1:10 'He fled from the Lord's presence'. How can you escape the inescapable? It is like throwing a crab into the sea and expecting it to out-swim that sea. The wayside pulpit message said 'If you feel far away from the Lord, who's moved?' As he fled, things were thrown from him. That Shalom had given him was lost in the rush and push to get away. Three times the word 'fled' appears in this book 1:3,10. & 4:2. The Revised Version puts it into the present tense as if he was still running away from God. He certainly was. The faster God ran towards him, the greater was his speed to get away. Only one will slow down and it isn't Him who has all breath. It is a likeness of the horse leaping over the fence and galloping away being chased by its owner to no avail. It is another cameo of the spent arrow flying aimlessly through the air without a target just waiting for the final drop to the floor. The hand takes the fallen arrow, not to snap it but to re-feather it and use it, wiping the mud from its point of entry, into the muddy earth.

If God sends you into difficulties and the floods begin to rise, He will have an ark ready prepared for you, each room and level is there to contain some consolation. If the Great One sends you into a stormy sea, the right ship will be provided.

The cost of burying your talent is great

When a Minister was invited to a church, they requested him to come, but stated he would have to pay his own fare. The man went to a service, and prayed that God would speak to him about this move to the new church. The preacher was speaking from the book of Jonah and he said 'If you are out of the will of God, you will have to pay your own fare.' The listener thanked God and never moved to the new area. Was it the will of God?

William Cowper was suicidal. He wrote many of our best known hymns. 'God moves in mysterious ways His wonders to perform' is one of them . In depression and feeling suicidal, he called for a coach, intending to throw himself from some bridge. It was foggy. The coachman took him, he got a little sleepy, and without knowing where he was, but knowing any place is good enough to commit suicide, he wanted to be let out right where he was. He left the coach, and to his amazement it had stopped right outside his own home. He went inside and began to write the hymn we have already quoted above. If he had succeeded in committing suicide, what a great talent would have been wasted. His poetic words would have gone with him.

Something happens to us while the talent is buried

When we unearth that buried, allowing the word of God to do some digging and breaking that fallow ground, we find that buried has been re-invented. The sheer effort of uncovering it, and lifting it from where we placed it high or low, has built us into a proper person. We feel that qualities have been added while it was in the dark. It is easier to manage. It is easier to use and be used. No, the answer is the child you were when you hid it, has now become the adult who comes to collect it with relish. There has been some things added, not to the gift but to you. How often have we looked at photographs taken at different ages, and seen the remarkable changes without knowing it. God has filled the vacancy of the talent buried with a new light and strength. New music seems to sound out from it. If it is some musical talent, the instrument can now reach the deeper notes, finding its way into new scales. What we have to contribute to the Kingdom is worth something. In that darkness of being lost and thrown to one side it has found a new lustre and cutting edge. Nothing now requires to be forced. It has a natural instinct for service. The way ahead is full of open gates as opportunities. There are more stirrings in the heart than in the eagle's nest. I can now do all things through Christ who strengthens me.

We make fruitless searches away from God for peace

They in the ship wanted calm. It didn't matter what it cost they wanted things to be calm. Nothing was required to disturb them any further. Finding calm is not always the answer to a concealed consecration. It only allows you to continue forever more as a world without end. A calm life is no indication of God's will. What was a more serene picture of tranquillity than this seaman asleep in the side of the ship. There is the calm of deadness and lack of challenge. There is the calm of the vase set in pot. Flowers painted on canvass look very calm. They are unreal! Calm things do not always promote peace of conscience. The same word 'calm' is found in Proverbs 26:20, where it describes 'strife'. There can be disturbances even in our happiest moments, because without God and going His way we have stormy weather even on the calmest of days and at the brightest of sunsets. The secret is to be as the oyster or the muscle in the shell. The sea may be rough but there is always a sense of security when we are inside of another protection as we are in the Almighty.

Horatio Spofford was travelling on a ship with his wife and four children, a contented family. They were nestling in the very presence of Infinity. The ship sank and all the children were lost at sea. After that dreadful dark night in the midst of day he wrote the song 'It is well with my soul'. 'When peace like a river attendeth my way, when sorrows like sea billows roll, whatever my lot, Thou has taught me to say it is well, it is well with my soul'. Francis Havergal, an old writer of the last century wrote on a piece of paper 'Once the will of God to me was a sigh; now it is a song'. There is a prayer from the Island of Iona, said and sung many times when they needed help to worship their God. 'Be thou a bright flame before me, be Thou a guiding star above me, be Thou a smooth pathway below me, be Thou a kindly shepherd behind me, be Thou a real friend beside me, tonight – today - forever'. He will be all these things to us as we take up that cross, for balanced upon it are all the talents of God, the Greatest One being nailed to it, to rescue what we have in God.

Notes

1   Jonah 1:6-8

2   See earlier chapter 2

3   One of Jacob's sons

4   John 20:26-28

5   Genesis 37:5

6   The Septaugint Version. Written for Greek speaking Hebrews

7   Numbers 27:21 1 Samuel 28:6

8   David Livingstone the missionary to Africa.

CHAPTER 13

The using of your talent without sacrifice

Every man sacrificed unto the Lord, Jonah 1:16. Jonah was counted in among those who made that supreme surrender but there is no mention that he was prepared to restore to the Lord that fourfold which had been taken and hidden.[1] If it had been given, it would have been heaped into his bosom as that multiplied many times. Like the good seed in the parable of Jesus.[2] Even in the midst of sacrificial worship, the talent can remain wrapped in a Babylonian garment as some wedge of gold. While other hearts are bubbling over I can be as cold as stone. There are some things we are prepared to do, but of equal significance there are other things our yielding does not include. It only includes that not infringed upon. There is no immolation with a talent disposed of. Half buried is all buried. You cannot even serve two masters. It must be "all for one and one for all".

When we sacrifice it is all or nothing

If we only use part of it we surrender no part at all. Why use one string when we can use three? There is that danger of being partial when we should be impartial. Working and serving includes all I am, and all I will ever be. It is an investment, which is born out of investiture. The out-working of that sacrificed in real fire is another way of speaking of devotion. There is no yielding when a thing is buried. It might as well be a stone or a piece of broken pottery, buried in its own shattering. Buried so low as to be deeper than the centre of the earth, and bypassing hell itself.

The hand of God is always there to help with sacrifice

There was a Hand awaiting, the same hand created the worlds, waiting and wanting the change to be given back after the spending spree, but nothing is proffered, and therefore, nothing is offered. It becomes a mere husk, and a thing like a cobweb of no substance. The tokens of that consecration are found in consecrated acts, like telling the sailors about the living God. The initial evidence that sacrifice has been restored is to get off this ship, and take the first opportunity to go and do what Supremacy has said.

They can be that buried in the ashes of a former existence, and to bring it back and be used by the Adonai is like entering into a re-incarnation. This is like the drawing up of the ship's anchor or the unloading of its cargo, little at a time. There has to be a rebirth of fire in our breasts. Fire keeping us warm when surrounded by wet sea and icebergs. These men of the sea sacrificed to the Lord, and in doing so disarmed themselves completely to this Master of the Seas. Jonah wasn't ready to see the former plan brought back into action. The very plan that he had sought to fragment with the hammer blows of a steely heart. All was not earth or anything representing a solid mass of achievement, it was just as foam in the sea, being swept along by the slightest change in the wind, assisted readily by a change in the current. These sailors were willing to offer up what they were. If you are going to be used and useable then you must be available for further training before reigning. 'If you offer all your faculties as a living sacrifice' (Weymouth's translation of Romans 12:1). Further in the same chapter, in verse 11, you read 'maintaining the spiritual glow', (Moffatt's translation). That 'glow' will be maintained buy giving ourselves to God,

There is further education through sacrifice

There is another school to enter into apart from the School of Whales. The fees are sacrificially high. This happening to God's Prophet was a part of the 'Finishing School.' That given to you by God requires to be surrendered just where you are. You learn your best lessons and receive the deepest teaching in the depth of where you are. There are events and happenings around you seeking to stamp impressions upon your life, causing you to bring back that taken. At the point of contact it has to be given to the Owner. There must not be a delay for more favourable terms or conditions. While he delays that around him is being rotted away. The teeth of salt in the sea are acting as mice. There is a nibbling away. Things that we are involved in will change until change and decay is all around you. The One you serve is the only permanent thing in both this world and the world to come. There is a demand to take from the coffin that buried, and restore that dying of its native breath, by letting God kiss it. It is quite simple to build rainbows as coloured umbrellas in your dreams. They have to be made out of substance and mean something as God's rainbow did and which was an arched thing as the sign of a covenant covering all the peoples of the earth. Its end touches nowhere and everywhere, that all might shelter under it. There was a certain calm about maintaining what was 'status quo'. In that sacrifice, we are melted to be moulded. Every sacrifice teaches us that we can be accomplished in God. The hand of God is the altar on which we offer the sacrifice.

Sacrifice is never easy but it is thorough

They made sacrifice look easy, because they did it without thinking about it too much. There is a Bible verse that speaks of giving, and when you do it, do it with 'simplicity', do it without thinking twice. If you think too long, that thinking twice develops into a whole army of reasons why must I give up this, that has been given to me? If you think a lot about it you are really building another ship to replace the one about to be lost. All that you have and are was meant for you and lent to you by the Creator just as the sun and moon lend their influences to land and sea. These two become the very voices of nature sounding out near and far to valley and mountain.

There are principles of sacrifice seen throughout the world that you live in. That can be so buried as to accept no responsibility. It is easy to go through certain rituals, doing what is expected of you, as this man among men did. No one else knew the difference between what the seamen offered and what Jonah kept back. It isn't what is offered, but we keep buried what measures riches or poverty. Your giving and sacrificing is measured by what you keep for yourself. Others were true while he was untrue. We withhold so many things even in our sleeping hours, which comes back to haunt us in the daytime. There has always been the thought embedded in the word sacrifice of destruction. Destroy the old to bring in the new. Let little ships receive blows and buffeting that will sink them so that the new thing might be launched. That new thing will herald to the world all that you are. The name of this ship is 'Sacrifice' and may God bless all sailing in her. God once showed me the picture by the Holy Spirit of a floating raft held together by ropes and nails. The wind blew upon it, and as it struck a rock, a whole flotilla of boats emerged from the broken wreck. Each vessel was a lifeboat. What He breaks He makes more out of.

The Church is the essence of sacrifice

There are so many sacrificial saints in the Church of Jesus Christ. Their surrender is weakened because they do not give 'where they are' and they do not give 'what they are'. I was once going to have to make a decision. A number of openings were presented to me. I was measuring one against the other. Then I read a scripture which opened my eyes and restored my peace of mind. The verse said 'You shall not offer your sacrifice on every altar, but at the place that the Lord has commanded'. This was the place. God was at the place where these were freely and fully offered. The one who seems to bury and therefore limit everything he touches did the same with his sacrifice. It could be offered anywhere. It might as well be offered now. It never left the altar as a ship never leaves the harbour while being refurbished.

Partial sacrifice puts the fire out

If we give here a little and surrender there a little, the whole thing becomes weak, and the buried talent is never fully restored. They didn't wait for lilies or fair blooms to begin growing out of planks of wood before they subjected themselves. They did it here because they were told to and because they wanted to. They offered all they had. It has to be offered where the voice speaks to us. In Genesis 22, Abraham offered Isaac at the place in Mount Moriah where God spoke to him. The package is no good without the present. The past is a poor offering for the present. What had been frustration and fear, what had been a very difficult time, as a ship coming apart at the seams, they had it all taken away to be reformed into something quite new and quite different. As for this sleeper, as a door being closed and a curtain being drawn to keep the light out, so is his heart in these matters.

More is added to our sacrifice

What they gave to God came back with more added to it, touched by the hand receiving it, and sending it back with a blessing tied to it. Even when these men were fishing, they threw a worm over the side of the vessel, in a measure of small obedience. It returned with a fish clinging to it. Knowing that when we give anything to God, He always adds to it. If the Infinite had asked the man with insight to do any great thing he would have done it. There weren't a thousand new things the Lord was asking for. It was the doing of an old thing. It was carrying it through to completion as the fruit of the tree goes through seasons until it is fully formed and fully ripe, so good that you eat it. It fills the stomach, pleases the eye, and gives new strength.

We can remain untouched by the sacrifice of others

The flame of their devotion never melted his heart. All he was left with was the smell of burning. It was Peter who denied the Lord before an open fire.[3] Jesus died, and in the resurrection he met with Peter on the shore of lake Tiberias by a fire that was burning.[4] There was new fire from old ashes. Things that were not offered on the first fire in the temple and never could have been were offered on the second fire. Something has happened to the cousin of this son of Jonah. Nothing died for him and nothing lived. It all had stopped, and he was going to leave it where it was. A cold sea and wind had chilled it into a freezing death.

There are certain pains involved in sacrifice

It is willingness to the point of pain that reforms lives. It turns dark doors into open windows. The pain becomes a field for freedom and delight. You can love God and do what you want to do. When the unrepentant turns to the word sacrifice in the dictionary of the Theology of the Spiritual, he finds it has been expunged. It is but a blank space, and unwritten upon as upon his heart. It is as that virgin and untouched. He could make it with just sacrificing without using the deposit of gold in his life. Why use that depicting the finest and the best when he can offer that maimed and blind as they did in the Book of Malachi. The two together, surrender and sacrifice meant double application, and that was far too costly. He had paid his fare! A definition of an offering and a sacrifice is that of the apple and the pork chop alongside of it. One is but fruit while the other cost a life. It is found in fish and chips. The chips have never died as the fish has.

The sacrifice in Jonah 1:16 was made to Jehovah, as if they were saying you kept your promise, and we are keeping ours. Jehovah the God of the long journey and the tiresome way. There are some promises from God that are buried as rings on the finger of the dead, when we allow our richness to be turned into poverty as refuse. That flaming from the given would act as a stairway to God. When Jacob had a vision while he slept of angels ascending and descending down a broad stairway.[5] One child said 'Some angels are descending because they are malting'.

Sacrifice matures what we are

When we do resurrect that given we bring it into such a large sphere. The reason Jonah failed and the reason you have failed is because you wanted it to operate in the area and arena of your own heart. There is that within all of us desiring self-control and manipulation. We will go if we are the drivers but we make poor passengers and an even worse spare wheel. We feel we must be part of the action. Once we come back to God, we are set free to let that serve in the whole area of the heart of God. It surfaces in God. There are so many things in the heart of God towards us. The flame on the altar releases a sweet smelling savour, a picture of the willing life. It is a ship, which is perfect, that means it has all its compliment of sailors and all the sails are bellowing in the breeze. The holds are full with treasure, and they are transporting the king who is going to be crowned.

Jonah could have made an offering without its throat being cut. We can offer that bloodless, and the grain offering can be that gathered from the ground where it fell. This was what happened to Cain before he murdered his brother.[6] That was offered which didn't really die, and if it did there was that rolling off the altar before it could be properly burned. It was only half-baked. It is not the giving of the leg, the arm or the head it had to be the whole. When it says they 'sacrificed' it does mean a holocaust. It was as full as it was final in that they offered the vital ingredients, but not this servant of the Lord. There was the giving of the ashes without the animal.

He offered something else for sacrifice

He, when asked for his hand and heart, offered one thumb instead of his hand, and offered his mind without his heart. An empty body with no heart and with only a thumb. That is not bringing back to daylight the thing buried in darkness. When they were about to put a missionary into the pot, and kill him. His resolute answer was 'That is alright, I died long before I came here'! The word of John and Betty Stam when they were being killed was 'To do by death what life could not.' If there is the element of surrender when the need for the supreme sacrifice comes, it is not as difficult. The sacrifices we are called to make, make us. They are written in red blood and not in yellow streaks. This sacrifice meant many different things to so many. To you it might mean taking the cover off that covered up. It can be the sacrifice of forgiving where you are. It can be one of praise where you are. It can be a sacrifice of love where you are. It has to be 'where you are'. That adds blood to it because it is not easy. The blood on that sacrificed must not be allowed to run dry. If it does, then offer yourself in a deeper way in such a way that it makes the former sacrifice only look like the squeezing of a grape.

There is great depth in sacrifice

The very lamb that the Israelite family had to offer was raised with them. If became one of the pets of their children. The day came when they had grown so fond of it, that it had to be put under the knife where they were. If this man offered a grain offering he might have been thinking that he would starve to death in the open sea for he had given in the grain for an offering, what might have been a meal; if it is the last supper, have it with Jesus. Think of all the many things that are sacrificed to form beautiful coral in the sea. These men wanted a port that they could direct the ship into and God freely offered that safe refuge to them. That meaning 'Dove of God' would come in, but without that he had been told to take with him. In the sacrifice of the dove one was killed while the other was set free.[7] He thought he was permanently the free one. He stands before the altar with the full hand behind his back; the empty hand is stretched towards the altar. He says the required phrase. He knows all the jargon - he has been spiritually brain washed. The watch or clock will never give you the correct time without yielding its works and hands. He reminds you of the way in which they used to 'win their spurs' as knights of the Round Table. If one came back from battle, he was sent again to come back when he had some scars. These scars are the hard decisions we are called upon to make. There can be a re-birth of those first balmy days of first love for Jesus Christ. Get so close to Him that what has happened in scripture, where the apostle Paul says, 'I bear in my body the marks of Jesus Christ', Galations 6:17 The very scars of His hands appeared on the bodies of those who would yield. You might have only been offered blood, tears and sweat, but those objects can be turned into a crown in the battle of life and the battle for life.

That sacrificed must not be self consumed

That sacrificed must not be eaten. It must not be self-consumed. The wine must not be drunk if it was a libation, a drink offering unto God. When we bury our possibilities this is what we do. We send that below which should be up on top. That is placed at the bottom of the pile instead of being as the flag on the top. That designated, as captain becomes crew. There is an association with the barnacles clinging to the bottom of the ship wanting a free ride. There is such a contrast between the Water Lilies and seaweed when we try to offer bloodless sacrifices.

When the Persian soldiers complained they could not break through the enemies ranks. One of their leaders went to where the battle was most dangerous, and presented his body to the swords and spears of the enemy. As he fell, his body became a bridge that they stepped over to gain a tremendous victory, proving it could be accomplished. The example had been set, and they poured themselves into the mould.

That taken from God and held prisoner can never set others free. Jonah is as bound as a nailed plank. He goes where the ship goes, not where Destiny tells him to go. That will always be a burden to us until it is offered to God. When it is offered it will grow. Sometimes it grows wings and lifts us up with it. Sometimes it appears in a new form. It is a burden tied to the ass's back. Unlike the yoke of Jesus, which is 'easy', meaning 'well fitting' with no chaffing.[8] It helped the animal to pull the plough with comfort. It fully fitted and accomplished that what it was designed to accomplish. We can develop our talents by giving them back to God. He wants to make them a reflection of you. We are not made less or weaker through our sacrifice but stronger. The one becomes the many. That defeated is turned into that overcoming. That offered is turned into a flame. The altar does its work as we must, and as Jonah should have but failed to do. This is not the end of the matter that is placed in the hands of God. There is much more to be developed yet. If He has trusted you with a plank of wood, next time it could be fishing boat then an ocean going liner.

That offered in sacrifice is very costly

There is such a cost involved in bringing that back into circulation, having allowed it to go into some secluded place. In 1 Chronicles 21:24, where King David uses the word 'cost' in relation to that offered to God, he uses a word which Jonah might have received and added to his empty mind. David the man who was the shadow of the substance of God's heart. It is the same word 'cost' found translated 'grace.' it is the word 'gratis'. It is that 'without wages.'[9] That carried out in work without expecting any pay. It is only working by grace. Grace God's riches at Christ's expense.

We have a phrase, which says when we work for God, and respond to him we 'work like Billio.' There was a Vicar called Mr Billio. He built a church being assisted by others, but working day and night with great sacrifice. All his talents were fully invested in the Kingdom of God. He worked so hard that the phrase was coined to 'work like Billio' meant to give it your all. Let it have your best shot. If the shot doesn't reach the target or fails to kill it, then throw your gun at it! There will always be hard labour for those who work to bring to birth. It was easy for the prophet to simply offer something he didn't want. Maybe the lead in his heart had become too heavy to carry, and it benefited him to release it and call it sacrifices. The great thing about God's servant is that he does come well in the end. 'Considering the end of their conversation' (the full course of their character and conduct) is a good New Testament adage.[10] The word 'conversation' means turning it up and down from top to bottom to see if there is a crack in the top or bottom. Looking twice in case you missed something the first time. It is the sacrifice and the action of giving back which unlocks the locked and digs up buried treasure. As the incense is burned, touched by fire it releases all the sweet smells locked up in it. There is always the element of lock, stock and barrel when giving to the Supreme.

Don't wait until there is no hope to give to the Owner. Don't say 'I will accept this darkness' when all is as dark as that without form or feature. If the ship is about to sink, don't even think about learning to swim. Don't do it under threat. There is no threat in love. It has to be done, not in a storm (even in a teacup) or while we are blown about, but in the calm of our own hearts. 'Reasonable service' cannot be reasoned out sometimes. In this we take shelter, God will only take what we accept. He can never take what is not offered. There is little grace in a clenched fist when we are giving. The word of God becomes a quiet place, and as we open it, that opens to us our responsibilities. If all your strings are loose then none will be attached.

One great sacrifice will make way for others

One great sacrifice will make way for other smaller services to take place and to find their place. There will be freedom of expression created for others. We are sometimes threatened because we have shoved things out of sight. If we would let God have them we would become examples, feeling no threat.

There has to be that balance as was found on the hem of the High Priest's garment of grace and glory. It was a bell and a pomegranate, a bell and a pomegranate.[11]   There was the music, the singing, the preaching and testifying, there was the service but fruit balanced it all. It is gift and grace that always work so well together, to make a song as they combine and become a duet of the Divine. We use the oars as the sailors did to row away from the challenge. You cannot sail away or row away from God, but you can anchor in Him. When sailing days are over there will be no sacrifice.   Paul fasted and prayed as he sailed, as recorded in the Acts of the Apostles, that book written for Holy Ghost living.[12]   Tomorrow will rob you of today. Excuses are thieves and robbers that break through to try and steal and kill. They come to take your best moments and hours as they came to the preacher sent to Nineveh.

Let the sacrifice be wholesome and deep

If you are going to build a memorial to talents and talented people, do not sketch it in water. Let the deeper colours of life come through, and let people see it for what it is. The Bible does not hide anything about the son of Ammitai. It tells the truth, the whole truth and nothing but the truth. It tells it as it is. There are no corners to hide around. The bed blankets are thrown off and the full light is switched on. The measure is that of truth and not tricks or trinkets. If you are going to build that which will last, built it into that which is lasting and longest, the Kingdom of God.

When we build an everlasting memorial we must start somewhere. Do as these did - start here and now. The first decision, the first brick in the building is the most difficult. The first chapter to be written in any book is always the hardest. Sacrifice is the largest measure in any Weights and Measures. This offered, cost them something, it might cost you everything. The word 'cost' is right at the end of Pentecost. It would have cost this son of a prophet his own way and what he wanted to do. There is an easier way, there is a shorter journey and that is contained in your heart as it goes straight to the heart of God. Every heart must have a place for another, but this was not so for this man, and is never so for the person with the shrivelled abilities, when fruit is turned into a branch.

Sacrifice is when a thing of quality is being offered

There is an old saying among the Greeks 'Never sacrifice a white cock.' This was supposed to be connected with the moon. They were saying don't offer to God that which is not the real thing or that of quality. Jim Elliot the missionary to the Ecuador Indians was so right when he said 'He is no fool who gives what he cannot keep, to keep what he cannot give.' Is Jonah listening? When they made an appeal in a church in South Korea, a woman came and gave her only rice dish, saying she could eat without it. This was the only thing of value she possessed. The secret was, she possessed something which did not possess her.

As you open your heart and hand to give, what you give, make it as big as what God gives. You know, whale-shaped, wind-shaped sea-size. In the open heart of God there is more than the hand can take. There is that withheld which can only run over when it is pressed down and shaken together as Jonah was in this wind. That one simple act can say 'rejoice with me, that which I had lost is found'.[13] It can put a ship back on course. How many people were going to be influenced when Jonah brought that out of darkness into light? When he began to operate in love instead of in his own spirit.

In Japan when any Party wins a General Election they dot the eye. They complete the picture through that one act. As we surrender there is a completing of that required. It might only be the dot in the eye missing, and yet it is missing. That buried, as iron will be given back to you as gold. When God is involved 'the iron did swim'. Up from the murky depths the borrowed, talent came. Back to the hand that it came from, 2 Kings 6:6.

Sacrifice will always put something into you

There has been a process while that has been buried. Unseen and unsung but it has been happening. It isn't a different talent that we take back. We sometimes think it is so good and new, why did we ever surrender it? Why do we let our abilities become tarnished with the years? Allowing lost moments to paint them a different colour? It is not the gift that has changed but the operator. You have grown while that has been planted. Many a little child has grown enough to reach the top shelf, and they have thought the shelf has been lowered to their height. They have grown without knowing it. There is a need to see ourselves, our abilities by the light of the fire coming from the sacrifice. If only Jonah could have realised this at the moment. It could have saved him from such a lot. Some of God's time could have been saved for you and me in His dealings with us. There is a limelight, which comes from the fires that burn within. Nobody wants what they have been given to be turned into foam or salt. If God's choice is taken and used we would light such a fire as will never go out. Future generations will live in the light of it. You will become the light for the turned page. All it takes to set it burning, is a spark of desire from your heart to the heart of God. Many waters would not quench it. Ability is a rare crown. Light from that given would have shown a pathway to the heart of God. The pathway to the heart of God would have run through his heart. It would have been there as the plank of wood running the length of the deck of the ship until it reached where the captain stood. There was a mote (a plank of wood) in his eye, stopping him seeing correctly.[14] Not placed there by God, it could have been all the same inside and outside.

Striking a match is not having a fire. That potential might never come to birth and mature until, and unless, this man of the Book decides to take that belonging to God and give it to his Master. There has to be a new willingness to 'go' and 'be'. When we have seen where we are in relation to God, then the next step is ours. As we move, we bring that with us, long-lost and forgotten, in acumen.

Notes

1	Luke 19:8	5	Genesis 28:12	10	Hebrews 13:7
2	Luke 8:8	6	Genesis 4:3	11	Exodus 28:34
3	Mark 14:54 See author's book	7	Leviticus 14:6,7	12	Acts 27:21
4	John 21:9	8	Matthew 11:28-30	13	Luke 15:6 & 9
		9	Jeremiah 22:13	14	Matthew 7:3 & 4

CHAPTER 14
The methods God uses to rescue your talent

Everything is beautiful in its time.[1] It is beautiful even without time. It is even scented beauty at the right time. Time is used to keep it to a certain date when it happened. I have seen pictures on the faces of watches and clocks, of beautiful flowers arranged on the hours. You look at the time as the gong sounds on the hour to see what you never expected, a lovely bunch of flowers! The right moment gives it a beauty all of its own, making it unique. Each finger of the hand of God produces beauty in so many forms, far more beautiful than hammer, chisel, paring knife or sculptor's tool has ever produced. What He does is as beautiful as any flower ever shown.

The shattering moments can become shared moments

Even those shattering moments of life can be turned into that shaped into a step. It is a step upward, forward and onward. The timing of God is unto perfection. He bends the fingers of time to point to our time. He bends things without breaking them just when and where it is need. God steps in at the right moment. If you learn to share whatever shatters, you will discover a rare beauty in every incident. It will never be an accident. Some chapters of books have their opening words placed within a bunch of flowers. God says things to us, and allows things to happen to us, to develop us in new ways. There aspects of life which are dull, they need something adding to them, that only the unexpected can add. That sudden addition does far more than that calculated in the coldness of the human cranium. Between the happening and the hurt, He is there. Where a shadow is, the Great Time Keeper steps out of the shadows, they become the substances of sunshine. When this Master Tactician and Technician comes, it is when we require the help the most. The New Covenant writer speaks of it as being in the 'nick' of time.[2] God coming to us with a view to help us. The right time is part of the happy hour of first faith and love. It is when God comes to rescue the gift and the recipient. To do it He will move heaven and hell, earth, sky and sea and all that is in them. When God steps in, He makes large footprints, and in those prints, talents of years of burying are taken from their seclusion, and displayed as trophies of grace.

Jonah was given help and help is granted to us when things go wrong. When we are broken God comes as that whole.

God acts silently and royal

That done by God seems to us at times as the sudden changing of the traffic light or the small coin rolling unnoticed through the hole in the corner of the pocket. But it is all well timed by God. What he does is organised and yet spontaneous. There seems to be, to the natural man, the appearance of fragmented organisation. It might appear suddenly to us as it did to Jonah as the whale emerged in that part of the sea where he was about to be thrown. God turns what seems to be a tragedy into a throne, building that throne from stones thrown down around us. He rules in all areas as we saw in an earlier chapter. We can be caught unawares when Providence is dealing with our wares. That 'arrayed against us', can be arranged for us. The El Shaddai does not come in with a fanfare of trumpets. He makes a splash the size of a whale. He prepared his own submarine. Whatever realm the talent is lost in, it is found in One element and that is in the Ruler of earth and sea. God responded on a grand scale. The great fish responded to its nature and calling. If only Jonah would! If only we would! Nothing happens to us outside of the will of God if we are obedient and not presumptuous. God does the best in all He does. He never crowns your dilemma with a crown of thorns.

The whale was dedicated to what it had to do

This huge fish preaches a message of gigantic proportions. It has obeyed God using all it is and has, and there is plenty of it. That huge mountain of fish is totally committed to its cause and the cause of God. The prophet should take lessons from it. When God rescues us, He plans silently for us in love. He can do it in a big way as He did with Jonah. Some acts of God are hardly noticed. When He moves as other times, it is through a display as large as a whale. There is great learning here and great response to the command of God. At the acceptable time, at the right moment, God does the right thing. There is the right movement, which brings it into line with angels who serve God. Everything about it symphonies as some great orchestra with everything blending together. If the fish had arrived to do the will of its Creator with its mouth wide open, using what it had in the best possible way, if God hadn't acted as he did,

Jonah would have still been asleep. It arrives as Jonah strikes the sea surface. There is the throwing of one and the sending of the other. That sent by Jehovah prevails over that thrown away as garbage, it always does. This sent was to become the potter's wheel and the carpenter's bench, and the penitent's stool.

What God does is for our teaching

God in seeking to bring back that taken from Him and hidden, uses a miracles as a cook might use many dishes. They are all here for our learning. They are introduced that we might come back and give back what we owe. Given back with 'usury'. We owe a debt we cannot pay, and God pays a debt He did not owe. In the preparing of the whale were the ingredients, the very recipe for preparing this man. It was one tool to engrave another implement. There were such large abilities in it but those in this runaway were so small and shrivelled to the size of a speck. The greater to teach the lesser some lessons. What a large school it was. A group of whales is called a 'school'. Going to school with whales. There are large lessons to be learned by you and all as we read, stop, think and listen. Hunger will drive the whale after small fish, if only this hunger could be the seer's hunger for the spiritual. This whale speaks a language that we need to understand. Not all God's messages are prophesied through prophets. It is doing a work for Him who sent it. It is one thing helping another. The helping of the lame dog over the stile and the assisting of a prophet over a sea and back to where he should be going. After God had schooled him and scolded him for a while, he would travel far better carrying all the weapons of his warfare with him. That lost in battle needs to be retrieved in another battle.

Experience makes a man what he is

Thrown into the sea as a sailor, he comes up as a fully armed soldier. When God baptises us, He baptises very deep. While down there he received everlasting impressions. There are things said to him in that world he listened to. He would never listen while sailing on the ship. His soul was deeply marked. Alone, not in a cave or on a mountain, but in a whale with God.

Yet, God did prepare this fish but the most difficult thing to work upon and alongside is the heart of a man. Within that heart is a whale, but not like this one controlled by God. There is no problem with Jonah in the whale. The problem is the whale that is in Jonah. Rebellion and resistance can take on huge shapes. I knew of a man who used to wear large shoes and big hats to impress people. There is rebellion here beyond the measuring rod for it can't be measured. So great that Christ has to come and die, not for fish or creation but for Mankind. There is a talent here shelved in rebellion. Put into a glass case for show, when it might have been doing the same work as this monster in another realm. There wasn't anything extra-ordinary in God sending him to 'that great city'. It is what we make of what has been said whether we bury the talent or break it. That message sent, unless it is taken and mixed with faith by the recipient, will seem as cold as the sea around.

God mixes the paints he bring to our lives

God mixes the paints He wants to bring to a believer's life that He might add colour. Left to our own choice, we choose only one colour. God has many on the palate that He takes His paints from. He has mixed the right colour to add to your life. Different Psalm hold different colours which require adding to us. Psalm 23 has a certain green of restfulness. Psalm 22 has the red of redemption which we certainly need. Psalm 51 is the Psalm of repentance and we need the black from that. 2 Kings 3:22, we require the red from the miracle figured there. The blue and all the colours of embroidery found in Exodus 26 & 28 can be placed into your life. They are brought that no life might be just black or grey, even black and grey. God knows when to add the pink, the red and the yellow. He so mixes them together that they provide another texture. Look at the waters that are used. All the happenings in the life of Jonah are mixed as paints with these waters. God wants to paint as some artist, a full picture, in full colour, of the talented man full obeying God. He would like to paint him just as he is entering the gates of Nineveh and preaching as he goes. This before us is the first brush stroke with the tail of a magnificent fish. If only this man's desire for so many things might be mixed with God's love for him. The great fish only took him as deep into the ocean as he had buried the gift of God in his heart. In all the turning and twisting of this huge mountain, living mountain, acting as some lathe, the prophet is turned inside out and upside down. God made where he was running from into where he was going.

God prepares all because he is prepared for all

You can never catch God off balance. He is so balanced and equal, that He upholds all things by one word of His power. His preparations are long and deep. We only ever see the action, but not the motive. We may never see the finished article, and until we do, we have to see only 'fragmentary portions'. Every part, and every phase of the life of Jonah needs some preparation. We think God has finished when He has only just begun. Jonah, as he appears will only ever be the prophet in the making. What will God make of him? A thing most rare and willing obedience. God tried so many times to bring out the quality of obedience in him. Most of those prepared by God failed, and that is why He had to send Jesus. There was no failure in the arrangements. The one man was as much trained, as a whole army might be trained. God is not training him to fight but to surrender, then go to war. Great is the diversity and university of the Teacher when dealing with the multiplicity of the human heart. You will note that where the talent and the talented one were placed, no matter how low or how far out to sea, God was there to speak to him, and he spoke to God. There was no hiding place just an abiding place under the Shadow of the Almighty. Each happening and thing devised became a finger on the hand of God pointing the way to bring that back into full view. God 'prepared' what his man wasn't prepared for. That word 'prepared' suggests he prepared it as 'mercy' found in Psalm 27:7. When God prepares, He does it on such a grand scale. When He goes fishing He takes His fish with Him. He always finalises something big like heaven, salvation and hell. God used something that already existed. He didn't cause this whale to appear out of nothing. He could have done that. He wants us to realise that out of that hidden away, he wants to introduce it into something big. As the whale was larger than Jonah, so are the talents and purposes of the Almighty. He ordained that to sink lower than the seer to lift that up deeply earthen.

He arranges things as he does the stars and flowers

Wherever we are, if it is hidden we take it with us whether on land or sea. God arranged this as one might count the number of stars (Daniel 12:3., Psalm 147:7). All the parts must be put into place to effect this rescue mission. It was as if there was the arranging of an army (1 Kings 20:25). He organises it as well as the accountant organises his figures. At the end of the miracle, at the bottom of the column it all adds up to grace and help given to reinstate the crown, which has fallen from the head. It is the crown giving the head its value. Be careful where you place Lordship. It must go to the source of Help. Do not give any acclaim to the ship or the sea, not even the whale, but to God the giver and maker of all these things.

God sends his special messengers

This large fish was sent by God to the very area and place that Jonah was thrown into by the other members of the crew. One, in Jonah, was operating outside the will of God, and he was just thrown in. The other, the whale, was sent by God. It is much better to be sent to a place than just thrown in like a pebble into the sea. Have your choice! The safest place in this kicking, spitting snarling sea was where Omnipotence placed him and rescued him. That hand to deliver is of a huge size. The Director of Affairs sent this Island into the sea where He knew it would be most needed. The whale thought it was there to fish. God is the One with the materials; He could send an angel in human form or a cherubim or seraphim. That sent in this record was best suited to water, a great fish. He could have sent the horses and chariot in which Elijah was taken to heaven God had other plans in His dispensation for in it He has many a sensation. Guilty of mutiny he meets his match. It is no contest. The monster has only to yawn, and the rebellious disappeared. He slid down into the inside of the whale. It was rather like descending into a coal mine. Just as a lump of seaweed he was gulped down. It was in the pile of buried seaweed that his own talents were discovered again, and he became a type of the resurrection of Jesus.[3] A resurrection, and being a type of Jesus had never entered the mind or the heart of the runaway. What seemed to be broken and shattered was patterned bt God to fit in as part of a jigsaw. When the Almighty wants to deal with a deep-seated ego, He sends the biggest and the best tool of his trade. It had such a big mouth it couldn't miss its object whatever objection he raised. The monster was as committed to swallowing up the predictor as any other thing it had ever swallowed.

In the quiet moments God speaks to us

Here was a cathedral in the sea. There was time to come here and reflect. In the relative quietness to hear the voice of God again. All the loose string being united. He was a lonely worshipper in the Church at sea. Jonah becomes the smallest thing in the largest thing in the ocean, controlled by the Largest Thing in the universe. When Majesty sends for men He sends big carriages. Their failures are covered with a large coat. He needed this large amphibian for the baggage he was carrying in his heart. If you want him to remember and receive a lesson, then send something big to shock him with. He attended a service here conducted by God on the resurrection. There would have been a certain loneliness and despair if God had not been here. Here, God could speak, listen and act at the same time.

The Book of Jonah is a Prison Epistle[4]

The book of Jonah is truly a 'prison epistle' it was written out of this happening in his life. How God sent rather a large life buoy to rescue him and all that was in his possession. We are witnesses to what happened. To get under a pile of rubbish that buries potential, a larger amount is sent to make a discovery. When he went into the sea area it was like looking for a needle in the sea, but God knew where he was. He knows the number of hairs on your head, and the number of feathers in a birds wing. God could have sent another wind. He could have caused a crab to nip him where it hurts. Even a shark or swordfish could have sawn through him. All of these things would have missed the very thing that Providence was seeking. When God is in charge, He gathers through a large basket in a whale so that the story, the drama might stand out in our lives. Big rescues take big things to do it. That is why Jesus came. There was no need to pull on the oars now. He had to let the fish do the swimming and taking. He has lost his independence. The Lord wants him to find it as he removes the wrapping from around that emblem of service. The talent is being restored and to do it, it is placed in rather a large casket. Each wave contains a drama for the escapee. His life has been as a wave. The sacrifice has not been there, as it is not, there is a wave being dashed onto the rocks to reform into another. He must grow while in the large fish. His prayer of chapter 2, became his prison prayer.

There was once a Shoe Firm who through advertising brought people flocking to buy their shoes. They simply put out the advert 'We are at your feet.' Another shoe shop wasn't doing very well at their business until one night they experienced a robbery. They put in their shop window 'People are so desperate for our shoes, this is what they do to obtain them.' Here is that within the feet of wandering Jonah which needs new footwear. Like Moses, he has gone swimming and he needs to take the shoes off his feet. The foot wear of the servant whose shoes tell of his position. His feet were now covered in slime and seaweed when they might have had the dust of a repentant Nineveh staining them.

There was more to the great fish than seaweed or blubber

A fish has been defined as that which vibrates. It moved Jonah's heart as it swallowed him. There is that having to be shaken until it is thoroughly mixed before it can be taken and used. Before your whale comes there must be a new depth. The tide must be in and things must have a flow about them. The size of this messenger over-rides any pretence. The biggest thing in the sea catches the man with the smallest heart. It was from whales that Engine oil used to come. The Eskimos obtain their light from the blubber. There is both light and inspiration here. If you read the Hebrew Herald that day, the headlines shouting at you would have been 'Fish catches man!' It wasn't a fisherman telling this story, and therefore it was enlarged. It was God through the inspiration of the Holy Spirit and telling it as it was. Jehovah Shalom had to get him into the place where he couldn't go anywhere else. Many pray when they have a strong conviction that they have no-where else to go. He was locked into the position of calling upon the Lord. Just as the ship on the canal between the locks. That whale became a sanctuary and an altar. It became the area of enforced memories. There was just something here going down into the spirit of the man.

God brings things of substance

An old proverb states 'They who climb trees must grasp branches and not blossom.' We must take hold of the real thing and be taken hold of by the real thing. He is being trained as to what the character of God is. All the Divine attributes flood in through those open jaws as wide as open gates to a city. He is learning slowly to let God work it out. He takes a back seat, and God does the discovering. There are things that Omnipresence wants to harpoon. God goes for big things with big fish. This talent which was part of Jonah meant so much to the One that gave. His talents are His children. Sometimes, they are the attributes of God placed in men for service. It was part of His heart, buried by a cold digging tool. Like a buried treasure ship it had to be sought after.

That failure seeks to cling to us

Whales have always been associated with the name of this sinking soul. It acts as a spur when following the Lord. If you go to Bedford Museum in England, you will see the very jug that John Bunyan's wife used to carry soup to her husband while he was writing 'Pilgrim's Progress'. If you visit a place called Rothwell, Leeds, England, where there is a meeting of the ways, there is a seat for you to sit upon. Arched over that seat are two bones taken from a whale. They are placed there as if to suggest when you are making any decision think on this man. There is something so deep and large in Jonah that even being swallowed by a great fish can't bury it.

That provided by Providence doesn't take us for a ride. It takes us on a journey where all our deserted pathways merge into one. It takes us deeper, away from the shores and shallow of our destiny. We are taken until that denied is re-tried and found not wanting while we are waiting. There are some so impatient with God that they would have used any minnow passing that way. They grab hold of the first passing fish or thoughtful suggestion. We must wait for the real thing to diffuse something of itself in largeness of capacity into our hearts. The fish was on a greater course than any ship. It was sailing in that mapped out by God.

You can avoid shipwreck

Avoid the rocks and reefs by allowing yourself to be taken into deeper waters that will wash away all your faults and wasted years. Only Deity can gather the wasted years as wool from the shorn back of the sheep, and weave it into something so comfortable and acceptable that you begin to wonder how you ever managed without it. When this man went fishing with the children of Nineveh what a story he would have to tell them! We have all seen parts of sunken wrecked ships above the surface of the water, left there to warn us. They are usually found in shallow waters. That great monster with all that inside of it is but a drawing, a masterpiece of the heart of the one inside of it and praying for deliverance. This became his school of prayer. He learned how to obey again and how to pray again. Here he was taught a vital lesson of how to avoid calamity.

It is better to pray than to wish

It is better to pray than look all around for the wishbone of the whale. He re-entered the will of God in a big way. Not now at his own charges or fare paying, but with God doing the arranging and paying. This large object was so well fed with fresh fish. God doesn't put His finger on that buried potential; He sends a whale to it.

There was a young man who went to Doctor Billy Graham to tell him that he wanted to leave college, he was tired of waiting around and wasting time. Billy Graham replied 'If you were given a blunt axe and asked to chop down trees, surely you would stay until you have sharpened it.' He who was so small is swallowed by something so great. It was into the depths of hopelessness and despair that the thing received went. It was found a lodger, but only until he had learned a few 'home truths.' God shows how committed it was. His love is even greater and fuller than adding whale and sea together, they are but thimbles compared to His love.

Coral reef has no such beauty as God wants to form in you

Coral reef has no design when matched with what Shalom is doing in the heart to revive the dead. There is that as some plough hidden in the clod. It needs to be brought back and harnessed to usability until it shines. It is never the years you have kept back from God, though, when added together they are the size of a great fish. It is not the disappointments of the same stature. We are over-comers when we are brought to dry land where we commenced going astray. There is a returning to this One after there has been some shovelling and digging in the human heart which can be as some graveyard.

Notes

1   Ecclesiastes 3:11
2   Hebrews 4:6
3   Matthew 12:40
4   The Apostle Paul wrote a number of epistles from prison.

140

CHAPTER 15

The talent receiving new power and opportunity

One of your many talents is that ability to pray. It is only one of the knives in the cutlery set. If this chief of gifts is absent, then all the braves will be missing too. With prayer we have confidence and defence. This ability to pray ties knots. When things have been broken it puts them back into their proper order. They are all marshalled in prayer as troops ready to do battle. When even that deposit fails, prayer and pleading will not fail. It stays the faltering feet. When any person prays, they are asking for help. God is that help. From the prayer uttered, new power and opportunities can be ours. That blunted and bent can receive a new cutting edge

We are all called to pray

If you can speak then you can pray. Yet, God had to place Jonah in the belly of a *great fish,* as the New Testament calls it, and in the most adverse circumstances, before it is ever recorded that he uttered one syllable of prayer. This is why there are no people without abilities, all can do things for God. All God's children are born with this silver tongue ministry. If you are training children, if you are a parent, much of the ability to deal with children is born in you. This is the parent of all the graces. It is not only a gift to be able to communicate readily with God, but it is only one of the grapes of Eschol.[1] There are so many things given, but none should be isolated from another. Each thing given should be complimentary to the other. We tend to emphasise what we feel is best and greatest, but God never does. A man never speaks in other tongues better than when he prays. They are all that is best to Him. He works one alongside the other. Each oar of the ship was dependent on the other. The prayers of each person become a whole rope to somebody in need.

Praying had no priority and therefore no ability

Pleading before God was at the bottom of Jonah's priorities so he never prayed until he reached the bottom of the ocean. Rock bottom, as we strike it has a way of evoking prayer. Oh that Adam's family might plead at the top of the ladder as much as they ask at the bottom and on the way up! Or, at the top on the way down, and they want God to become that other rung in the ladder to stop their slide from dizzy heights. Seeking God is seeing the same and it would have saved him from shipwreck. Instead of the down, down feeling and happening, there could have been a constant ride over the waves of this water. To pray is better than a known way. It is fuller than an ocean and more direct than a missile. In adverse circumstances we make some marvellous discoveries. Such discoveries as things are not where they should be. It is at this time that the human heart is exposed and expounded. Being cut wide open, and we realise that there is nowhere else to hide. Trying to hide from the Almighty is like you placing your hand in the air and trying to hide all the fingers there. We are as that in open water. On the surface of it for all to see and bear witness against us. Each moment seems to have a voice to shout at us. The pointing finger is towards us. That in the conscience is as a cutting blade. I have fallen on razor blades. The man in the whale begins to feel convicted, this cutting will set him free. How Jonah must have felt when swallowed by something so large as a whale. There were torments below and above. Yesterday and tomorrow were all shut off from him. Barred from him by this hulk of blubber. He could not reach out with his hand. What he couldn't do with his hand he did with his heart. He began to pray to the Master of this prison inside the whale.

In prayer, having no friends to help, we discover an old Friend

When he couldn't talk to anything else, then he spoke to God. Abraham Lincoln, a former President of the United States of America, once said, 'I have often gone to God in prayer, with the firm conviction that I had nowhere else to go.' The old proverb says 'Some doors are closed, some doors are open, but the door of prayer is always open.'

We thought we could never do that! When seeking Jah has not been your lifestyle, then it is very difficult to adopt it in a second. When we pray on a regular basis, and it is recognised as one of our many talents, we always have a safety valve. We are like a child with the alphabet. What we have been taught we use, but not with jumbled words. Jesus helps us to take the single letters born out of pain, and make heart-felt prayers of them. This sort of intercession comes through long hours of training. The Eternal One was as gracious as Jonah was open in that He listened and answered the prayer. We have the listening ear of the answering God. This Jehovah put His part of the covenant into practice, and He always will. When we have as many holes in our side of the bargain, as the very nets we fish with. When we are as dead as that uncreated and as that still yet to be, the Supreme Being will perform for us acts of creative life to help us. He will bring two parties together. What you have not kept as this runaway, God keeps his part and sees to our part. The fish become as some strange altar. When and where there is no hope, He creates hope. It proves you can call upon God as your friend, wherever you are. Years ago if we ran out of any provision we were always directed by Mum to go to the friend next door.

To pray is to take your second opportunity

There is that opened up before us leading to a 'second opportunity.' It is to breathe in, and take in, the wind of God that gives new inspiration. This proves that when we need God to revitalise that given to us, He will breath new life into it, as He breathed the 'the breath of lives' into Adam, (It is plural in the original language). Genesis 2:7. This is the language of love and of the heart that contains healing virtue. This is no 'smash and grab', it is part of the plan of gentle persuasion by God. It gives a new edge and point to that held within our hearts. Solicitation opens up our hearts wide, for the hand of Jehovah Jireh to come and grant a new dimension to what we have. Long since hid, but He revives it with a special kiss. It is a kiss of wonderment to us for we didn't expect this. Infinity chooses some of the most unconventional and inconvenient places to bless us and restore us. He speaks to a whale on Jonah's behalf, and it listens to obey. The fish responded.

Prayer reminds us of lost promises and opportunities

Sometimes we have to sink low, very low to rise high. There is that within us, planted by the Lord, as it was entrusted to the prophet Jonah. It took extreme happenings to bring Jonah back from the sea in which he had been ditched. The great fish didn't have to intercede but Jonah (not the son of a prophet) did. The heart needs to be made bigger than the influences that bind us. God is wanting to lift you high after being brought low, to bring you in after you have been tossed out. That laid aside needs to be taken up again, God knows where you left it. Help is at hand because God is the Lord of the depths of the sea and the dry land. You cannot be where He is not Sovereign. It wasn't the jolt on reaching the bottom blunting the sharpness of the gift, but the rebellious heart of the prophet was being knocked into shape. The salt of senseless thinking had been doing its eroding work. It can sink a ship and take to pieces and fragment metal. It works in the human heart. He was making it less and less useable, and, therefore making himself less responsible. Notice Giver and gift were never separated, as operator and Giver were not segregated. They were together in this. Both were in the problem, one was part of it, but the other was the remedy for it. The sinking one claws his way through seaweed and slime, using prayer. God is only ever a prayer away.

Prayer opens the plans in the hands of God

God has plans in His hands. God in seeking the one, finds both, and puts new life and opportunity into equal parts. There is the balance of restoration brought back to his life. Prayer helps us to understand what God is saying, and to see what He is revealing. Before God steps in, all you have is a blank space; you can be a blank space that God wants to fill. It can be a silent picture, but God wants to add words and music to it.

At the moment we have never heard him pray. There has been no eruption of his spirit into a groan of prayer. There has been no deep stirring of the spirit such as when the tail of the whale smacks the ocean surface. That paining him has never been translated from pain to prayer. You can't get more closed in or shut up than that provided by the closed mouth of a mountain of blubber. God has a plan of escape, and it is prayer which promotes it. This which God was going to do was not formed by the seaweed into letters of the Hebrew language to be understood by Jonah. It came in response to a prayer.

In trial, try prayer

The next thing for the son of Adam to do is to pray. It is not even to go to Nineveh. To stop to pray, and to be stopped to pray is more important than going to Nineveh. There has to be the finding afresh of the pathway from the heart of God to the hearts of people. Prayer is that vital link, that vital bridge between the two. He has to discover that, to make his gift relevant at all. It is of little use offering to a choir a voice that can't sing, only croak. You would be better giving it to a bottle of cough medicine or even to a frog! Without a mission and without a purpose all the talents in the world are as pegs on an empty washing line or a frying pan with nothing in it, upon a very high flame. When in the deepest trial, stay and pray. Let prayer become your anchor. Among all the debris and ruin in the whale's stomach, he prayed. You can go to Nineveh later, but pray first, pray now.

There has been a vital link of communication missing. It is discovered within this chapter. There is that appearing not as something created or repainted, but as a longing re-designated and called what it is in simple term's - prayer. It is the yearning for Majesty. It is that letting go and letting God. It is not telling the One above us what He wants, but where the man went wrong. There is an inner self-healing through this method. It didn't take a long course of studies. The diploma at the end was the assurance and the knowing better of the Divine. This was to hear and understand what was being asked and said. It was the mending of a relationship, not between Jonah and the fish, but between him and the Creator of the hump. That prayer became the throne of God. It seated sovereignty in the problem.

Prayer is approaching God with the right attitude

It meant to simply approach God with the right attitude. In a few minutes the folly of hours and days were washed clean overboard. In a measure the physician had stopped being a 'quack' doctor, and he had healed himself. Drowned in depths never to be remembered against him any more. It is the child coming to the Doll Doctor and handing to him the doll with broken arms and legs. In this one's case, it has to be a broken heart. So broken that instead of blood gushing out, prayer leaks out. Rolled into that pleading is the willingness to be restored as the eagle. The loveliness of love is poured in such a gentle way. He is being called. Then he has to be sent again, but in such a way that he doesn't realise it until the final moment when the whale coughs him onto a beach and he lands facing in the direction of the 'great city'. There is the binding of the broken heart, but there is the winding of that heart around the heart of God. Then as God applies the certain remedy such as pain, hurt and frustration he begins to let those things through his lips buried deep within the human heart. The kink and the wrangling must go from the chaffed and chastened spirit. That whale became the workshop of the carpenter of Nazareth. God was knocking new nails of conviction in, and seeking to secure anything that was loose. That ready to fall apart and drift must be secured with prayer. Life is so fragile, handle it with prayer.

It is God who gives the interpretation to our prayers

It is an utterance in 'another tongue' with God giving the interpretation. What had become 'other tongue' to the one who doesn't pray is native language to God. He loves to hear the child forming new words in prayer. All the darkness, deep hurt and frustrations are poured out in that prayer. What is received in his suffering is placed as an offering before God. It is an awful happening, you create new things in prayer. The asking is that utensil that he carried those things to God in. In every happening there is a key to be found for your release. Prayer, like God, is always there. The whole of the second chapter of Jonah is devoted to prayer and the release of the prisoner to a place near to where he wanted to go, but had refused when Jonah ran away from God. He could have been coughed into that city where he had been sent to, but God leaves him short, so that he can make his own way. Somewhere between the beach and the city, something happened. All his prayers were answered. Jonah was the answer to every prayer he uttered, because he was the problem. As he goes the extra mile himself, it is proof that He has been listening for the moment. When he has listened to God he has heard more than he ever heard from all the crew and captain of the vessel. When spoken to, not many words are used. Words are not mixed or minced; this is direct talking to the heart. It is hammer-head striking the nail head, sending it ahead.

When ships sail they carry cargo and they take messages between nations. Even the flags that flutter in the fresh morning breeze have messages to tell. Prayer is such a thing as it is loosed from its moorings and brought out of its little inlet into something bigger, deeper and richer.

We feel that our prayers have no impact

His words are as wood as the staff of Gehazi being placed on the face of the dead young child.[2] It may bring a measured response, but it doesn't hand back to God what he requires. It doesn't open up all the doors of the heart to let a new dynasty in. There had been no fountain of the deep broken open so that this man might call upon God. What happened to him brought a flood of pleading from him and through him Jonah limited the success of all he sought to do. Prayer is the taking of every day language and letting it be interpreted by the Spirit of God. The fish might not have known what the prophet meant or was trying to express. The sea or the ship and other sea creatures certainly did not. The Master did. The ear that was listening and the eyes that were watching, alongside the heart that was planning did know. He is the interpreter of what we say, even when it is the wrong thing. He created languages, and sometimes there is a 'language barrier' even in asking and begging. Did he plead in his best Hebrew grammar? Sometimes it is not the words bringing us back, but the eloquence of the tears as they flood the face and add water to the seeds that are being sown within us.

Prayer is fasting for receiving

This kind of asking, you know the asking of prayer and fasting, must be a coal, a hot coal from the altar. There must be a flame of devotion in every word offered. God had to put some new interest into prayer, and He does it in rather a large way; by letting the man without prayer be swallowed up by something he can't handle. The greatest thing to handle is your own life. This he couldn't do, and the whale was even bigger at this moment than his life. It was the Almighty's full stop for the moment in the written history of a circling prophet. God can answer the prayer. The problem is what will Jonah do with that answer. Will he be answerable to none?

He has to turn to other means, that of prayer but it is the discovery of that long forgotten. It has been a long time coming, as long as a 'slow boat to China'. There must always be a lifeboat at our disposal. The distress signals founded on the famous 'Save Our Souls' are not the whole matter. There has to be that linking of the soul to God. Ropes tie ships to ports by the means of metal encased in concrete, and we have the means, the hidden means sometimes, of securing our berth in God. Just to rest is not to float away. Just being with Him is enough to calm waves and nerves. It is getting to know just how big your God is. Prayer answered is your talent used.

It is so easy to pray when all is tranquil. The calmness of that moment can enter into the prayer. That is called for when the going gets tough. If we have a gift at all it is not designed to be a fair-weather operator. If we have any endowment at all it must be tested in all areas, and opposition must come from all quarters, and like Jesus Christ it must still arise from the dead. He must be awakened to the situation. There must not be the folding of the hands and the constant resting in a stupor. God sent the whale, as an answer to prayer, on a mission. To deliver a 'wet'* prophet onto dry land. Doesn't God have a funny postal service? He delivered Jonah to his destination, but he used the belly of a whale to accomplish it.

There is no prayer in a yawn

There is no prayer in a yawn. God brought him so deep so that he might discover just how deep he had buried that committed to him. Within each word uttered there is that giving new power to what many might consider failure. The failure is taken and re-applied, and it does not remain under the word 'failure' it is translated and placed under the successful things of life. The ability to pray must be aroused and kindled into that sparkling fresh. Before the Creator can put something new into it, there must be a seeking and a finding, before there is that transforming by the power that creates drops of water and huge whales. There were plenty of words on the tip of his tongue; they just needed to take a dive with him into something larger and more useful. Thoughts must be turned into asking, then asking must be revolutionised into taking and plundering. Each word had expression of what had been placed within him, which was retarded, held back until it became that able to operate. There is the possibility of prayer becoming as that never born. There is nothing like the wholesome cry of an infant child. Prayer is part of the birth pangs of obedience.

Prayer is always there when required

Each prayer has "Abba, Father" found deeply rooted in it. It is the putting of the hand of the crying child back into the hand of God. It is bigger than the whale or sea. Then we go for a walk, not alone, but together. We are together and everything is together. Not a breath is now between us as we arise with new boldness taken from the past failures.

* In modern politics, a person is considered wet, who does not toe the party line, or one who is always complaining.

There were certain standbys. Some things were there for emergency use only. The electric pumps are there to be switched on when the waters flood in. The modern computers can soon re-route and warn us. There are tarpaulins laid ready to do their protective work. The response which God was trying to rouse was missing. As time elapsed the distance between Jonah and God increased to the size of an ocean. The deeper the fish went the further away he seemed to be. Then there were stirrings in this heart. That hibernated became a thing of all seasons without reasons. The inside of the great whale became Jonah's prayer chamber and cathedral. It said that wherever we are, prayer could operate. God can hear prayers that are uttered deep down. The monstrous fish cannot take you beyond the hearing of Elohim.

There are many words that define prayer

The words used and suggesting prayer are found in Jonah 2:1,2,6,7,9,10. It is this sort of revived dexterity that proves that wherever you are, sovereignty can be discovered. It is God below the water as above the water. He must play the game by a new set of rules. These rules did not include men pulling on oars to take him to his desired haven. They did not even include the captain of the vessel, but they did include prayer and seeking God for a way through. He has tried almost everything else, now he tries answers to questions without reasons. It works where others leaked water. Where other methods sank, this sails on right into heaven. Here are nine verses given to prayer. That is nine times better than it was. If a man attempts to light his candle and fails, he must then continue until it bursts into flame. This prayer is saved for us in that offered for sale found in the big object. The opening words of the prayer are found in Psalm 120:1. They are scattered throughout the Psalms as seed sown into future generations. When any pauper or beggar lets their coinage slip, they will know to pray. When the talent is frosted and placed in the days of autumn, we can take it and bring it back into a delight-some land. This prayer is better than roses or a rosary. It was just what was required when inside the tummy of an over-grown monster.

Prayers to be uttered when in desperate situations

It should have been written into something suggesting prayers for different occasions under the heading 'Prayers when you are in the belly of a whale'. Finding yourself in a large hole that you cannot get out of, this prayer could be and should be used. The prayers of Jonah, chapter 2, can be used when we feel we have come to the end and the bottom of life. Jonah didn't have to use a ladder, or claw his way out. He had to let God do the answering, while he did the asking.

A whole chapter is given to what happened when he found his tongue and native language. He was able to use his Hebrew language to express all the feelings of his heart as some master musician might use an instrument to make you cry as you listen to such smoothing and stirring melodies. The prayer could have become one of the Songs of Zion, sung by a son of Zion. We must not pray to the situation. The water of the watery grave must not wet his prayers and turn them into that unacceptable. There is the possibility of them being turned into seaweed. In this new discovery that surrounding was being harnessed by prayer. That wild and large was being controlled from within. Jonah and God were working together through prayer.

We should pray before we faint

Luke (the physician's Gospel) says men should always pray and not faint, Luke 18:1. It is suggesting that men should pray and not 'cave in', being the meaning of the Greek for 'faint' in Luke 18:1. Jonah 2:7, 'my soul fainted within me' but not in God. John Calvin commenting on this verse says 'It means to hide, to cover, it signifies to fail'. My soul is rolled up. I have hung my boots up is the modern expression. This is as if a cloth has been thrown over the fainting form. The cloth was some size! The size of a whale. His soul did stutter and splutter as a fading and failing car engine, when the drive shaft has broken. When we pray, when we discover again our true potential for reigning prayer becomes the alternative. It is another way through. The ensnared did not have to commence carving great chunks of blubber out of the side of the whale. There was the ability to look outside and see heaven and the throne of God. That vision and knowledge is worth many large fish, a whole sea of them. If this created as a huge fish and sent to help will listen to God, maybe Jonah and you will. In the listening there was the intensifying of the desire to call upon the name of the Lord. That Name is larger than life, and it makes great things dwarfs. We must ask, seek and knock using the knowledge of the situation. This will sometimes bail us out, but it will also add a lost dimension to you as a person.

Don't cry over spilled milk, pray over it

Don't cry over spilled milk, pray over it, and just maybe it will turn into cream or a cow! In this attitude he reaches a new altitude. The situation is seen as the Sovereign sees it. Jonah tells it to the listening One as seen by human eyes. God sees it all, knows it all, and yet, He longs to hear it all bursting from your lips as a blast from any bugle. It can be what the trumpet was to the walls of Jericho. These walls were not thrown down. They had to be lived with until an appointed time. It was such a large answer when the whale opened its mouth to swallow but it spat out instead. What was inside of it was thrown outside, just like this intercession should be. When we call, we incorporate another angle which helps us to control what is happening to us. This helps you to see it from all sides, calling for help from every side, and that help comes from Him who is at every side and everywhere. Man has not discovered a place where God is not. That is why without this sort of prayer we are naked, blind and cannot see afar off. What the captain had been to the ship so this communication with that Presence is to the character of the Believer. This Rescuer heard above the sound of the seas.

There is no sound greater than the sound of a man at prayer

There is no sound that can drown out the noise of a tear when offered with strong crying. He heard from outside because He was always inside and at the side. The black blob swallowed down that thrown overboard, but it also swallowed prayer. The ability to be a winner was discovered by a loser. The tide was turning. This King Canute could really hold the sea back. Walled in on every side by the same monotony we discover what had been lost. The essentials of Christian Life and conduct are found and taken hold of once again. This utterance to God became the new starting line. I say this because in the old King James Version of the Bible the word 'up' begins to appear in the narrative.[3] This sort of begging should have been the first port of call. It was at the bottom of everything that the new discovery was found. There is that locked within, as a man inside of a fish which was pushed out to God.

We all tend to let the circumstances decide and dictate when we have nothing to pay with. We do have something to pray with. It is better than the wishbone of a whale! Don't let that around you turn you into a pinch

of salt. Let it just turn you until your eyes are fixed on your Master.
From this position all things appear the same.

Through prayer we can look out

Through intercession we can look out. This was better than the
crow's nest on the mast of the ship, which had sailed far away. The
prophet could cling to it no longer. Here he is clinging to God, as those
fish with suckers cling to the rocks. Believe and receive; so that the small
might become large and the large might be made small. Better prayers
never came from a much larger congregation. They were never uttered in
a larger building than this one. There wasn't much to distract him here.
There was plenty to keep him awake. This was the lifeline. There was
no reserve.

Prayer discovers a presence in the place of no return

Prayer discovers a Presence in the place of no return. This action
places hope as a beacon where there is no hope. It sees tomorrow
through a blank wall. It whispers assurances into the heart, when the
mind is full of doubt. This is his only lifeguard. When faced with a leak
we cannot mend that is the time to utter the heart. Things seemed all out
of place to the man who was out of sorts.

Jonah prayed twice. When he prays in chapter 2 and 4, there is the
thought of a new shoot appearing and rolling back the soil in chapter 4.
The other time he prays in chapter 2:2, it is likened unto a trapped animal
crying; or the cry of the parent animal giving a warning shout or cry to its
young offspring. This man is saying 'Lord, here I am, come and save
me.' Prayer is more than fine words or phrases, it is finding God. Prayer
helps us discover our self worth.

Prayer leads to discovery and recovery

In answer to his pleadings a hole wasn't made in the side of the beast.
God didn't lessen the size of it. He had to come out the way he went in,
but a better man with his experience. He came out displaying the ability
he had been given. The Supreme Being had some more work to do with
him yet. As the whale coughed or spewed ('sicked,' was a child's way of
saying it) him up. There were things deep down in this rebellious person

that required to be brought out of his spirit, and to be spat on the very ground that Jesus in the New Covenant wrote upon with His finger. There was that in the spirit of God's man which needed spitting out, as the whale spat him out. He came out better equipped, as a man he has found some of his manliness and manners. Prayer has pushed him to the fore. It has been given its former place of prominence. It becomes the chief operator. The opening through prayer has been created. He can begin to serve the Sender again. A blow has been struck for freedom.

Prayer is both messenger and message

Jonah 2:7, Adam Clarke commenting on this verse states 'There is a fine image here of a messenger going from the distressed into the holy temple.' Prayer is not shouting at God. It is not even telling God things He doesn't already know. It is letting Him know what we have seen, heard and understood. It shows that we have been moved and that we care. Care enough to share. Care enough to tell. Prayer is sometimes interpreting to God what seems to be the foreign language of the heart and of the spirit. Giving him the interpretation of our situation as we see it. It is in the time and tide of trouble that this brought back from the dead is able to help us. Your greatest talent might be just speaking to Jehovah. Where the throne is established in intercession, the King isn't very far away. He is even seated upon it.

Prayer is asking and receiving

Jonah 4:2, the word used for 'prayer' means asking and receiving. It is a rod with a double hook. There are two sides to it as there are to any coin of the realm. It was never meant to be one-sided. You doing all the asking and God doing all the listening. There has to be a place when there is the receiving. So many have a one-handed prayer life. They are like the man with the withered hand in Matthew 12:10. The garment which covered the heart of the High Priest had to be doubled, Exodus 39:9. There has to be that extra, double feeling for others when we pray. There are those who constantly as God for things, but never receive anything. All this took place when Jonah was unceremoniously tossed onto the beach to find his feet. It stopped the ship lurching and pitching.

When he was tossed into the sea as some fishing net, he went in with nothing. He had something but it was hidden. While there in the depths he cried to the Lord, that hidden was revealed, and he used it splendidly.

A small prayer can influence great things

A small prayer to make a large fish cough. Jonah had found his real rudder for sailing. The forgotten was suddenly remembered. A man becomes the next thing on the menu for a whale. Kingdom is what you are. The fish would eat everything in sight and it swallowed this thing floating in the water. It would have destroyed him but for God. There was that part of him no monster could devour. There were talents deep within him that God was fishing for.

Prayer is looking again to the hand of God

Jonah 2:4, he says 'I will look again'. This time I will see and hear what I missed before. How many things through lack of prayer do we miss? Then I will do what I failed to do the first time. What I cannot see, and did not see, I will see. This is part of the covenant of my heart. What I cannot and did not hear, that will I hear and listen for. What I have not reached out to touch and take from, I will reach and touch. Taking a fresh look means taking a fresh step. This will be examined and all that is part of me will be surrendered. Raise the flag of surrender by using your tongue! They have preserved the door of the prison where John Bunyan was kept as a prisoner for twelve long years to remind us that God answers prayer, and uses a prison experience such as Jonah's . His epistle was not as the book of Jonah, but what he wrote was called 'Pilgrim's Progress.' We have kept all the evidence of God's dealings with Jonah through something bigger than a whale called the word of God. This prayer was the first amenity to be brought out of his heart. If the God of the sea continues to fish how many other things will be raised?

Prayer produces a way in and out

There was the first thing to have ever escaped from a whale. God opened the door through prayer. He proved that where there is no way, He will make a way. That way will be as large as the open mouth of the sea's largest monster. It is when we are crushed low and swallowed up by the many things of life closing in upon us as great jaws that we can prevail. There was no forcing of the way open. It opened of its own account. It exhibits what can happen if we give that part of ourselves our gift, and take our hands from it, placing God's hand upon it. It was as much a miracle as ever being swallowed by this Leviathan.* You may touch the stomach of the fish but you will never touch the bottom, south, east or west of what God has for you.

Praying is putting God in charge

To pray is to place the Creator above the created. It is to put Adonai back into His rightful and regal place. It is to take from hiding the things that are abiding and true. It is to find your Creator nearer than hands or feet. He is there right by your side. When your eloquence has dried up like a tear, and it feels as if the Sahara desert with its many camels, humps and all, have been deposited in your soul. It is prayer that changes all this, and the silver eloquence of prayer returns to speak again, to tell it all to the listening One. Asking needs to be deliberate and desperate to the point of boiling over. It must be better than the foaming of the sea. As he was spat out, so does the problem need to be thrown away never to be found on any other day.

Prayer takes us through it all

Prayer will take us through the facts of life and living. It may not alter, as the creature was not changed as to its size or nature. A little girl, who had just taken an examination at school, heard that prayer could alter things, changing them so much, she thought she would pray. This was heard coming from her room 'Dear God, do make Paris the capital of Sweden!'

It was a large prayer from an enlarged heart that was offered. It was larger than could be copied into any prayer book. The answer was even larger. This type of prayer isn't read but it is said, with deep feelings.

Prayer is seeing broken strands woven together

Jonah took and weaved together all that surrounding him, and like a child weaving some daisy chain with bits of grass added. He weaves

* The Leviathan was a large sea creature mentioned by Job, which might have been a whale, Job 41:1.

around God a beautiful prayer, allowing that One to take the weeds from it, and present it as full and accomplished. The broken and smashed is pieced together as if it had never been broken.

Something has been added to him of worth, and you can tell that as he prays. This is where that which was lost is found. It is the commencement of rescue operations. It is found, and in the finding is the working and keeping. It is the first of all we see recovered in his life. This is a foundation stone and from this he is able to build wide and high. He can build from here to that city he has been called to. This stone which this builder had rejected has now become the head of the corner.

Prayer will lift you up, standing you on your feet

The actual physical position of Jonah in the belly of a whale we are not told. There wouldn't be a lot of space to breathe out a prayer. The next time we see him, Jonah having done all, stands. He stands now, not as a sailor, who walks leaning from side to side, but as a trained soldier, he stands firm and true. He arose and went up to Nineveh. He could no longer go to Joppa, but he could, and did, make a fresh start. A good thing appeared out of a bad thing.

Notes

1   Numbers 13:23,24   3   Jonah 2:6.3:2-4
2   2 Kings 4:29

CHAPTER 16

The cure for complaining and talent forsaking

When any person hides what should be shown and known they enter into the Kingdom of Excuses. They have more reasons than reason itself. We muffle that meant to be shouted into a whisper. When we hide our talent it becomes as the Manna that the children of Israel failed to gather at the appropriate time. They didn't use it during the time allocated and it bred worms and stank.[1] There is nothing worse than that talent buried and it breeding worms until it stinks. All around us know long before we know it's 'gone off'. It has degenerated never to be recovered again. We get taken up with the worms, and not the work. The smaller becomes more important than the larger.

The former things can be recovered as they return

There is a beautiful expression of the Scriptures the 'recovering of its former fullness',[2] describing man's role on the earth. They had to help God in its recovery. All they had, what God had given them in creative acts, had to be taken, and fully used. Even the first Adam, sinned and sought to bury what God had unearthed from the very soil He used for Adam's creation. God is able to do this with all our bitterness and complaining nature. He can turn grubs and worms into beautiful Dragonflies. They are multicoloured and have a ministry which is part of their lives, and they add to the world that they live in. They don't complain about the character of the One who made them and allowed them to be born into mud at the bottom of a pond. Use what you have while you have it!

There is a certain caustic condition produced when we run away from one thing and land in another. We intended to go by the street called 'Straight', but concluded walking along the 'Crooked Mile'. What should have been wine is turned into another by-product of grapes, vinegar. All the ministry of God to Jonah was rolled up and crumpled like a piece of paper, when the message written on it doesn't matter any more. In his complaining he demonstrated what we might call a crumpled spirit of complaining. It is just as easy using your own human spirit to turn water into vinegar and because the miracle is missed - there is no wine. There will only ever be wine while Jesus is consulted and included. When the miraculous hand is missing, all of Him is absent. We are left digging by things we say and do, but we neither know why we are digging or what we are intending to bury. The burying we do is to cover ourselves. We lay to rest our God-granted opportunities. That sets the soul on edge. It only arrives there as Jonah arrived because it does not remain in the centre of God's sweet and wholesome will. The one worm sent to help becomes the many worms of self destruction. If only we have obedience the size of a worm, we shall accomplish much.

When we forsake the cross, attached to any benefit that we have we are left with the empty wood, the nails and the thorns. We never hear the voice proclaiming it is finished. Complaints and a complaining spirit is found where we lay that on one side we should be using. That empty space is filled with far more vigour with a complaining attitude towards all things because we have forsaken the One thing. That broken and left behind, as that dropped suddenly develops sharp, pointed spear-like talons that rip and hurt. Those sharp points are sometimes hidden in the feathers of our own thinking and we foolishly think that nobody knows. There is a thermometer as we speak, telling those around us what has happened. There is a meter that is being read. We dress ourselves in the sackcloth and ashes of a burned out experience. The experiment went wrong. In the explosion and expulsion that followed we breathed in clouds of bile.

We all tend to blame others

We tend to blame the wholesome character, and put others in the same blame, baptising them into it. Jonah became oblivious to his peril, and the fate which was awaiting him. He didn't fully understand what God was saying or doing. Not fully understanding can make us both bitter, critical. It is the wood trying to out-manoeuvre the carpenter. There may be some things about God we do not understand. In the very soil we have buried our enabling, that lacking can be unearthed even as we dig. As we dig we discover that there is far more to the nature of God than stars, sun, moon and seas. He has a heart that we seek to bury in the words we speak. When rarities given are laid low, we lay the Creator of them, low with them. In Jonah's situation it is the crew member, blaming the captain for the rough seas and the salty waters.

God is not with us for what He can get out of us, but what He can place within us. That being given to us can grow until we know something of the fullness of the stature of Christ.[3] It is fullness of length born out of strength. This describes a statue, needing no additions, there is no part loose or missing. There is no wax added to cover up the faults from where we get our word 'sincere.'

Life is full of different moods even as clouds scurrying across the sky. The problem for this man was when mood swings took the place of miracles and the voice of God. We cannot put another idol in His way to hold sway in our day.

Some things are only for a short time

Some things are only for a time. They fulfil their mission as both Jonah and the whale did, but then we must move on to new things. If we don't, the old grows grey and less attractive. What is blunt and flat can become very sharp as circumstances apply their pressures to it until it becomes sharper than any two-edged sword. It is found in our complaining. When the Children of Israel complained, they dug their heels in.[4] They made a wedge out of the fact that they had no water, and produced a rift between themselves and God. The next waters taste in the wilderness would be Marah, bitter. They murmured against God. So many times we go under. That meant to lift us above, sends us below with a complaining spirit as a blanket for the cold shoulders of cold days.

There have been times when we have all complained. It means to sigh habitually. The Bible margin for Numbers 11:1 for 'complaining' suggest that it should say, 'We are at it we complainers'. One Hebrew word used for 'complaining' means 'to dig the heals in'. The word 'complaining' used in Numbers 11:1 can mean to weep. It is to have your way with tears. Instead of wrestling with Evil Powers we wrestle with that good thing given to us. We have sleepless nights when the light has gone from the experience and is turned into darkness. We, along with this servant, have allowed something to turn the light off and hide the switch. We are left wrestling with the goat nature. Both Jonah the son of Amattai, (Jonah 1:1) and Simon Peter the son of Jonas, had this sort of nature to contend with. It happens when we get taken up with what we wanted and planned. We all travel the Emmaus Road saying 'We thought it might have been deliverance in this particular way.' God doesn't deliver every convert by the hand of the Evangelist. He doesn't save one and all by the means of just reading the Bible. 'God has a thousand ways to answer prayer, and when I stand in need I know he's there'.

God does some lovely things for us

God has many great methods; the lovely thing is when it comes to delivering souls, all the methods work. Whatsoever things are lovely, the Greek word is 'very lovely' think on these things.[5] Think on a healing rather than an injury. Let the smile be king and not the frown. This man whose name suggests misfortune had the idea that his method was the only one that would work, and the Saver of Souls should have used what he suggested. It is quite amazing what God does, with twine a little bit of the thread that we think it should be His big ropes, when delivering people to set them free as happened in this city of people. A complaint as Jonah did, is a ram's horn and not a silver trumpet. Right at the heart of the bitterness, God was to produce honey in the rock. The nation of Israel held the record in one year for the most complaints received by any government in the world.

Great miracles do not alter human nature

The book of Jonah is the evidence that great miracles and deliverance for us do not in themselves alter our natures. It is the nature of the thing and the thing of nature requiring to be changed. The body may be changed in a moment, in the twinkling of an eye, but not a prophet of Israel. It takes much longer than this for the Potter to form up the clay and fill it with priceless treasures until like a scribe in the Kingdom, things old and new are brought forth. This takes longer than it takes a snail to travel a mile. Your heart is your market stall; wares you offer are shown in the market of every day living. Much of our doing wrong, is being wrong. Much of that narrow spirit has come from where we buried the talent in a narrow place. The flag of our devotion is carried with us for all to see. Sometimes it is a red flag, and at other times it is a white one. We see Jonah in his true depth and that is very shallow. He is found out, as he is compared with the God he serves. It is a spark measured with a whole day of light. That large and open spirit that was ours, it was so deep, so wide and accommodating. It has shrivelled from being a meter long. It has become so restrictive and narrow tapering into some

160

bottleneck. That has to be emptied from the bottle, and the neck cleared before new wine can be poured in.

Deep revelations do not change human nature

Revelations such as he had do not alter a man's nature. It takes much more than seeing a whale vomit or a raging sea calmed. It takes more than outward manifestations of God's power. It takes God Himself in Christ to sort us out, every part of us. To unearth some things and bury other things. Left alone, we bury the needful things, while we take up the hurtful thing, and to compensate we turn to Mark 16:18 'Any deadly thing shall not harm them', misusing the verse, almost turning it into a virtue.

To protect and console Jonah a gourd was created. God had sent the whale. Now He creates a living, growing thing reaching back into the sky as in worship to its Maker and Friend. When in the sea, God sends a whale. When on land He causes a gourd to grow. There was so much planted by the Jah* who became the Gardener. It came straight from the Garden of Eden with a ministry and message all of its own. 'Here is where I plant my flags in the shape of gourds.' This was brought from the Paradise of God. It was placed there as a faithful monument to the goodness of the One who cared. My care for you flourishes like this green gourd. Paul says in Philippians 4:10 'Your care for me has flourished again'. It has produced new green shoots of growth. He planted it right where it was needed the most. Just as this luckless one should have used that given by his Master, so the Planter plants that useful thing. He withholds nothing from this complaining spirit. When God does it there is a plan at work.

Negative complaining is bruising without healing

Negative complaining is bruises without healing. It is that replacing the very Gospel we are called upon to preach. Many a family after a church service, when members of that family have hidden their abilities go home to have a good moan before dinner, through dinner and after dinner. The best wine drunk in some homes is 'whine.'

In Jonah 4:1,2, He questions why this one was saved, and why actions took place in that manner. The child of grace becomes a tyrant of truth.

* Jah is an Old Testament name for God. It is a shortened form of Jehovah. It is found in Psalm .68:4

The one owing so much spends so much more than what he possesses. The dove of the Aviary Keeper develops claws instead of a sweet coo and gentle wings. There is certain vinegar contained in his speech. You can't wean God's children on vinegar! They shouldn't behave like that. You shouldn't talk like that. Look at the way they dress. Look what they are doing now. Does all this sound familiar, is it just sand or is there substance in what we have heard people say? You can bruise people without striking them with a hammer.

There is an over-spill of the heart. That has put to one side the very ability it possesses. It has turned its noble ministry into something far less noble. A far greater thing he could have done than what he was doing now. The man who made and sold locks boasted that no one could escape when they were fastened and locked in his chains. He was sent to prison one day. Thinking he would escape but realising they were his own work he could never achieve it. The servant of the Lord must be as his master; gentle, peaceable, kind and gracious, as easy as a dove in flight. There mustn't be the coarseness of sackcloth and ashes. God hasn't concluded the chapter of his life yet. He doesn't close the book of our dealing and doing (the book of our failures and history) until He writes the final chapter. As He writes, so His tongue becomes that of the pen of a ready writer. Jehovah believes to the last page that all will be well. His aim is 'without spot, wrinkle or blemish'.

If God had to complain about you

If the Judge of All had applied the same judgement to the man who buried his talent, where would Jonah stand? Where would he be? In many aspects of his life and conduct he was less of a saint than the sinners of Nineveh. That difference between the two sets of people was the hand of the Creator. When this murmuring streak enters into our hearts it seeks to cajole us into murmuring about beauty and goodness with the same mouth that complains about rebellion. It stains us with a yellow streak. The man of mistakes had one mouth and one outlook for all things, including the Righteous One. There is a story told of a child who was describing how mad another person was, when she said 'He was so mad and bad tempered and we could put up with that, but not when he took God's name in vain he hit God.'

If the choice was left with us

In that state of denying your calling and election unsure, what sort of people would be in your Church? You would choose all one sort. What if they all complained like you? Genesis speaks about bringing things forth 'after their kind.'[6] Surely we must not be as the surly? We would choose by taste and looks. This is what we are like when we have lost our destiny. We forsake the future for the present. That large heart that Solomon pleaded for, so that he could accept another with different opinions to himself. That heart understanding another's opinions has no need to become my opinions, if they don't agree with mine. The Abundant One is one of variety. The spice of life is found in variety. There can be that spirit of everything being the same. We might finish up with all cabbages, carrots or potatoes when there are many other varieties to be enjoyed by all of us. Who would care for a Garden of nettles or thistles? Whatever weaknesses I have, could become part of those around me.

Your ability and strength should be given to accentuate the positive, never the negative. When we have a talent it is the sheer joy of serving Adonai that keeps us from entering into the pulpit occupied by Jonah and imbibing his theology. There is a sheer exuberance in service that leaves well alone. We have that confidence that we can leave it all in the hands of the Master. Jesus said 'Let the wheat and the tares grow together.'[7] We may be surprised, as the preacher was, when he arrived in Nineveh, to see how soon they repented, and how this repentance touched each strata of society When the eyes of your heart are closed then you are blind to the inner prompting of God.

We expect God to be so long suffering with us

It will always amaze us how Jonah expected the longsuffering to be so patient with him while he was so impatient with God and other people. He did allow him to be thrown into the sea, but He never washed his hands of him. When he went into the sea some of the brine along with the fermenting seaweed, the tooth of a shark and the sword of the swordfish entered into his soul and spirit. He came out filled with these feelings. They were there before, but what he passed through, tore away the veneer revealing what was underneath all the time. When we surrender one gift we can take upon ourselves that not described as a gift, but as a spirit of weakness, as weak as the water we enter into. You have to be so careful that when passing through that experience you don't allow the bad things to enter into your spirit but the good things. When Jonah prayed in chapter 2, you might have thought he was an angel. Don't judge a person by their prayers, but by their practice. I once knew a parrot that could pray.

The darkness is not allowed that it might enter into us

We have been allowed to pass through the Valley of Shadows, not that the shadows might enter into us, and we enter the Dark or the Ice Age, but to let some sunshine comes in and we can reveal it to others. When buried deep, it is that dross might be turned into gold, that grit and hard stones might become precious sparkling riches. Covering up that given, we bury so many other things. There is a beautiful demeanour that can be laid to rest with it. When Lazarus went into the tomb, all that his name means 'The glory of God' was buried with him. When he was brought out, he brought things out with him that he never had before entering into that cave of death and misery. He knew that God can reach into death, and that He listens to the prayers of Jesus.

The grace of God is multi-coloured

Jonah 4:2, the word 'grace' or 'gracious' that he refers to and, on a surface inspection, seems to know a lot about, condemns him who is the perpetrator of limitations when applied to the character of the Almighty. The word 'grace' means to bend and to curve just like the rainbow. Here, he is trying to make the Creator into a straight line and a short line. You can't make God into a missile to be fired at people! We do things when we ourselves have applied limitations. We measure God by our own limitations, and not His expectations of us. God is not what we say He is or think He is. He is as far above our reasoning as the heavens are above the earth or the centre of the sea is from the land.. God has never buried Himself only in Jesus to arise from the dead. God is always the full picture and the complete circle. Sir Winston Churchill (a British Prime Minister) used to say of an opponent 'But for the grace of God there goes god.' If God is gracious you be the same. Don't tell God what He is, and then go and do what you are.

Grace reaches all and teaches all. It includes all. Jesus said 'As a hen gathers her chicks', and the wing of the bird is long enough and large enough to cover each chick. What a wonderful sight I have seen when three or four ducklings ride on the back of the mother as they sail down the river Thames. All that mother's abilities are surrendered to producing and rearing those young ones. There are no barriers in the love of Jehovah only in our hearts. We build fences through offences. That floods the human memory long forgotten and forgiven by God. We are human but the Lord is Divine. When passing through an orchard in Kent, England, I must not gather the briers and the twigs that would stick in my eyes. There must be no coming away with an empty wicker basket filled with just pips, cores or leaves with stalks. There must be the taking and partaking of the real fruit. Every happening is more than that. Happiness is more than happiness when it is converted into blessing by he hand of God. We mustn't put on one side our own way of accomplishing things, just as King David laid aside King Saul's armour, and picked up a small pebble from the stream. That taken in his hand from the stream was going to be used by God in Israel.[8] God seems to use the smaller stone rather than the larger armour of Saul. One scarcely covered the palm of of the hand, while the other almost cover the body of the warrior. Stones were there as gifts to topple the giant. He only took one thing to himself when he laid down another.

You are not the finished article

It is quite strange after we have spent so long as Jonah in the School of the Teacher, the moment we approach others we expect them to be the finished article. We expect of others because we ourselves have allowed something to slip. That essential part of us is not operating properly. We are as the one-legged man in the book of Proverbs, where it says 'his legs are not equal.'[9] There is such a thing as a limping spirit. The spirit of the Elder brother in the story of the Prodigal Son in Luke 15 is in Jonah. The Jews always seem to have this limited grace approach. God's hand is not shortened. There is no limited way with Him. If He reaches and touches one, He touches all in that universal He wants to reach and teach.

There is a sharp contrast between the words of the Man and His Lord in Jonah 2 and 3. Jonah 4:2 has been described as one of the greatest verses in the Bible. A God with that depicting no flies in the ointment.

There is nothing that withers, falls, fades or fumbles in Him.. God is as He is, because His attributes are never buried, when at the sunset He still shines. When the clouds gather He is still as ever He was. His years fail not, as a garment He is not folded away to be taken out and used on special occasions. He takes a full, deep look at the Master. What he sees buried in Him he doesn't like. What Jonah has thrown away, that spirit of largeness and graciousness, is not far away while God is near.

We give a picture of God to the world

There are always those who have hidden away their probabilities painting Jehovah using their own palate and in their own colours. We have a television programme in England where three artists are invited to come and sit near some scene. They have to interpret it into their own thoughts. They paint what they see onto the canvas. What each produces from that same scene in different colours and from different aspects is amazing. The Creator is not the creation or definition of any man, race or sect. If that known by this small creation could have tipped all he was into him. Like some great sea going into the open mouth of a great fish, then things might have been so different. When the fullness of Elohim comes rushing in it unearths all that is buried. All lost is found. The snatched away is restored. The time of the singing of the birds has returned to the soul in love, and it produces a dancing heart.

There are many ways of complaining

If we do not tell what is said or go where we are sent, if we bury that enrichment, then we are in a measure shouting at Deity as this small minded person was. This alone is another form of complaining. I must see things eye to eye with the creator of the eye. In seeking to protect and enhance the life of the prophet, the Master was seeking to establish and retain the evangelical spirit reaching out over the wall. Reaching out to others. That fullness flooding out into others. He lies down to die, and he would rather die than do what he had been commanded. For some to do what they have been ordered means death. There is a certain crucifixion for those who would serve willingly all the days of their lives.

Jonah 4:6,10 if we are not right, nothing is right. If we see things through a bitter spirit, all our red choice fruits are coated in acid. What we say and do just reflects the shade we are standing in. This is the reversal of 'rose coloured spectacles.' The church magazine made this comment 'Don't be surprised if you find mistakes in our Parish magazine. We print something for everyone and we know some people are looking for our mistakes.'

When the gourd sprang up as a soldier drawing himself to attention in the presence of his commander, it was Omnipresence saying 'This is a token of my presence with you.' We sadly can show more love for that benefiting us rather than that benefiting another. We are back to the restricted and restrictive spirit of the man. We make booths of our controversies. He might have spent the next twenty years living in the shade of the gourd, but the King had greater plans. There were larger trees awaiting him in Nineveh. That given to him as a gift was only for a time, and if we do not move on into something more or chop that down we were given years before and accept a new challenge, the Everlasting will send a worm that has the appetite of a hungry lion.

God sent new growth

That tree plant grew before his eyes as the love of Providence increased. The Immortal let something appear out of the earth. Where we bury things, He causes them to grow into their fullness. Do the work that this gourd has done. Be as faithful as this umbrella that has been provided. Do not make it the beginning and the need of everything. He is the Lord of the Universe; of forests and trees. Every plant is yours as part of His creative ability. Do not limit God to a little gourd or a small tree of experience. The cross of Christ might be considered by some to be so small, yet, God has conquered nations and kingdoms through its power. The Juniper tree spoke to Jonah's heart. It was telling him that God uses small things as they grow. It was only a small plant, but it held its ground in occupation. It provided shade for the prophet. This gourd can grow. It can hold its ground. What is an English oak but a nut that held its ground? What an inlet or some favourable harbour is to a ship this was meant to be to the soul of the seer. A piece of shade and quiet time to relax and reflect on the goodness of the Invisible. It gave him time to take up his talent again, and use what the Indivisible had given not in complaining but in reigning. Every promise should be a gourd.

The Essential came with what amounted to a bottle of medicine. This not in a glass or plastic bottle. It wasn't served on a silver spoon and carried on a silver platter. He will bring to us what He brought to the apostle John. The scroll that he was commanded to eat, which is recorded in the book of Revelation, was sweet to his taste but bitter to the stomach.[10] There are some things bitter to taste but they make us all sweet within. The will of the Eternal can become a hook in the fish's mouth. It can seem barbed but on taking it wholly to ourselves we find what we thought was bitter, is honey spread with jam.

The Revised Version of the Bible margin lets us into the secret of the gourd when it calls it 'a castor oil plant.' Here was the medicine for buried talents and a complaining spirit. The Doctor brings it to pour it in. You can't complain while the castor oil is being poured down your throat. It was from the seeds of this plant that castor oil was produced. The small happenings of life can produce the same, rich in medicine. Take the castor oil with a promise, the promise helps it go down easier. Jonah required so much of it as to need a whole plant or tree.

Dr Strong gives three suggestions as to what the original word for 'gourd' might mean.[11]

(A)   **It was an emblem of Jonah and his ways**

It grew in a day and then disappeared. It was here one minute, then the next day it was gone. The word for this plant is from a Hebrew root meaning 'to spit or vomit out.' You will do this if you take castor oil. It is as that with leprosy which failed to Redeem or be accepted. That neither hot or cold, and therefore it is rejected.

(B)   **It is a picture of the measuring rod of God**

It was only for a time. Manage a tree before you go to a city. The man who would climb mountains must climb ladders first. Everything is measured by His love. Here it is in a plant. This Sunshine brightens up the misery and the outlook with plantings. This rod was placed as a growing tree to develop son-ship, right there in the barren wilderness. He gives us the two sides of life, sunshine and shade. They are given to develop us. Adam began life in the shade of a tree, so must Jonah. This hapless one had been passing and was passing under the rod. You don't stay under it. There are healing qualities in it. It is the staff of the Shepherd. It is the staff of life.

(C) **It was a castor oil plant**

In God's provision there is that calling us into action. We receive what God has done so that we are as a strong man ready to run the race set before us. We don't travel light we travel in light. The Greeks always anointed their shields and weapons. God pours in this sort of oil. It isn't very nice to the taste but it does heal our complaints. Castor oil was known as the medicine for all complaints. It was the remedy for every malady. It is through this that the Lord purges out the old leaven. When God spoons it out the old disappears and the new appears. The castor oil plant is there for as long as it is useful. His medicine is given in large and small doses but it is always reserved for us when required. We must complain of our lack if that lack is home bred. If others can do it better and are more successful, then maybe, just maybe they have had more castor oil ointment than we have! Ministry was always meant to be complimentary and not competitive. If some nasty taste has been left in your mouth you need this refresher. Do not complain for it only took a worm to kill off the life of this plant.

Leave a place in your heart for new plantings

In your human heart, leave a place to plant roses, herbs and perennials but leave a reserved place the size of a footprint where Jesus can walk and plant the castor oil plant. Leave a small place for God to walk. Leave a place for growth. Leave a space for prayer and meditation. In days of depression and lost causes, in days of showers and cold you will need some castor oil to revive and refresh you. It can be taken with castor sugar.

The twist in this whole saga is that he didn't require this commodity when he was in the sea with fierce winds raging around him, but on a sunny day with the birds singing. It is never the circumstances but the heart of a man requiring to be changed. This may be the only growth needed to allow you to take up your talent again, and get back on track with a large intake of this castor oil.

Castor oil has its own medicine chest

Psalm 23:5 David records 'You anoint my head with oil.' All the healing qualities for hurts, scrapes, sores and bruises were in that oil flowing from the Shepherd's hand. When we have split apart at the seams and nothing seems able to bring the sides of the sore back together, to clasp one another in healing virtue Jehovah Rophi can do it as He did it for this servant. As the oil enters, the complaining spirit is healed into wholeness. The disobedience, tormenting and shrouding everything in mystery is chased out of the life. A life of misery can become a life of majesty. The oil can produce a missionary.

Notes

1	Exodus 16:20	6	Genesis 1:11	11	Dr James Strong STD,
2	Genesis 1:28	7	Matthew 13:20-40		LLD Exhaustive
3	Ephesians 4:13	8	1 Samuel 17:38-40		Concordance. Published
4	Numbers 11:1	9	Proverbs 26:7		by Baker Bookhouse,
5	Philippians 4:8	10	Revelation 10:10		America

CHAPTER 17

The second opportunity to use your talent

When one is multiplied by God, it doesn't amount to two. When God is included there are so many other miracles available to us. Five loaves and two fishes feed five thousand people. When the word of the Lord came a second time in Jonah chapter 3:1, the clock had been re-wound and things could be different now and not what they should have been in the past. The race was ready to commence again, and God didn't state where he stopped but the Almighty commenced where he was, as if he had never become short of wind. It was a new start but not with a new or different Jehovah. It was the beginning of something new, enabling the servant to take up where he had left off and what he had left off. He must not go, as a head without a voice or body and that is what he would have been without his talent. All his faculties must be as intact as was his Jehovah. All it had been to Omnipotence was a pause in the programme. In the past, God had been filling in a few details. The margins were being filled.

A new work with a new word

A new work done in His servant; he had to be made ready as any tree for winter, summer, autumn and all varying conditions of nature and grace.

The second opportunity was different because Jonah had now seen such displays as at any bonfire night of the capabilities of Providence. This was no Being in a framed drawing or painting. This manuscript of the Almighty had come alive. This One that he was serving was no bush that burned and then disappeared. There was no shooting star effervescence in God. He was no small change in the pocket used to purchase small things. Through the strength of all that he had witnessed as a faithful witness he could go and tell. Here was the opportunity for nobility to rise again and take up the challenge. God had erected an archway, like a bridge and on it you could read 'Ahead only!'

The longest, greatest, widest and tallest thing in the book of Jonah is the grace of God calling him into a second opportunity. It was his Master saying 'You may go and serve again.' All is not lost in the darkness. The tools of the trade had been shined into brilliance by the light of His presence. There should have been a fixed glow in his soul. 'There are rays of light that can be seen if your eyes are fixed on Me.' There are no great whales in Nineveh as he had been in the sea. This revival that is about to arrive needs a different approach and different methods must be used. Where it had been salt in the sea, there will be laughter and joy; great rejoicing in the thing that 'I Am' is about to perform. It will be greater than the gathering in of the wheat or the wine at harvest time.

The second opportunity

Opportunity to the Greeks was a bald headed man with a tuft of hair on the front, and the rest of his head was bathed in grease. If you missed him as he came towards you, there was no hope of catching him as he went by or disappeared into the future. He is a swift athlete who didn't wait to discuss times and seasons before appearing or disappearing. Opportunity has always been depicted in the turning of the tide. This is taken from the time when ships used the tide to move over the harbour bar. If the tide was out they could not sail. Here, for Jonah the full tide of The Invisible's love had come right to the doorstep of his heart. Such love carried the prophet to his destination regardless of the many obstacles. It is such a fullness as to wash away all the bad memories, and to take him leading the man not to jump over the cliff edge, but to come to that Solid Rock.

This opportunity was seen as an open door. The door of God's heart was constantly opening to this man. It had been wide open all the time, but for our sakes it is presented as some second opportunity. One might ask what did he do with the first opportunity? He simply fled and jumped ship to bury his acumen in the sand and the sea. When God holds the door open, no wind can blow it shut and damage that hand. With one hand He opens the door holding it, and with the other He gently coaxes the representative through. The word 'opportunity' can mean an open harbour. It was when the tide came in and a passage was ready for any ship to pass through with its cargo. It means the opposite to our English phrase 'in the offing' suggesting that waiting outside the port for favourable conditions and permission to enter into that port.

More opportunities with more grace

We can all identify with Jonah because God has given us more opportunities than grace if that was possible. He has come and we have gone so many times. He has pleaded, asked and told while we have remained as water in our listening capacity. We have had no ears for what He has said. Those opportunities have been more than the going in and out of tides. It is a matter of using our craft to be launched in our first love for Jesus Christ. God knocks not to injure us but to knock us into shape. God knocks not to bruise us but to heal us. That knock and persuasion is not to hurt but to open you up to all He has to offer. He creates a resurrection so that all lost can be found. That thrown away on the hillsides of life, He takes and gathers it together, bringing both us and our remedies back to where we should be, to go where we have been sent.

He hadn't simply locked up his opportunities and thrown away the key in the deepest part of the sea. When we lock things out of our hearts there is such a great need to have them opened to accept what is asked? When he threw away the key; Omnipresence caught it, took it, and used it to open it all up again. It is the same key not another or a new one. The key was not thrown back at the man. He might have missed it and it would have travelled too far from him to find. There were so many ways back to God for Jonah. This wasn't the one way of 'walking the plank'. All he had to do was to travel on the straight and narrow way.

When one opening closes another opens. It is always open to the Majesty. In fact that opportunity becomes many without being fragmented.

When the note is missing or there is some lack, Omnipotence can make it up. Giving to us far more than we ever possessed before. When we have lost our opportunity, God comes to us, not with that which we have lost, He has another expedition for us. His hands and heart are as full as ever. Without a new adventure the people of the city would never be brought to God.

The second opportunity brings no new word

It was not a different word that came to the missionary. There was no new revelation. He must take and use what has already been given to him. There are no additions in a second time. That which is already part of the baggage must be taken and used. New tools do not make better figures or carve in some more artistic way. The old ones are usually the better without being blunt ones, and that is why Jehovah has not taken another man to use to do His will. His will, we must realise, is not for creating a swing out of our mistakes, for us to become little children and spending all our days as a child on that swing. It is no slide or seesaw as part of the child's playground. There is a challenge and there must be the greeting of it as we go. There cannot be another word from the Lord until the previous one has been fulfilled. A promise given must be believed. What God has said to you about your gifting must be fulfilled. The 't' must be crossed and the 'I' must be dotted. This call and prompting was not to another field. God had not moved the goalposts. It just seemed to this human that the gate to the field had been opened much wider, in fact it was opened into all directions. If God did not close the gate, blocking the way to Nineveh, who did? This golden opportunity was not tapered to his fancies or foibles. Jonah was no carrier pigeon of the pigeon fancier flying back and forth, to and fro. There is no time to be scratching itching ears in the work or word of God. Go means go, it means shove and push, it means to force yourself to do the honourable thing. He should have gone, not as an uncertain sound, but as the trumpet sounding the charge into battle. He must not be as those on Mount Carmel that Elijah had to challenge. 1 Kings 18:21 'How long halt ye between two opinions?' How long will you hop from branch to branch like little birds.

The strength received in the former conflict must be taken and used more fully in what now lies before you as you muster your talented army.

What was all-dark is turned into light, the light of love and direction. His whole dark experience was flooded with light. His need was met at the right moment. God made everything fit together perfectly at the right time. He is the Second in the 'split second'. As the arrow flies, He can hold it in mid-air until the target is in place. Then it strikes where it should strike. He arranges both missile and target. The accomplishment is the greatest. He makes the best possible arrangements until all things are now ready.

God can suspend things until the right moment

Even between the oar strokes, there can be a suspension of duty until the right moment. When the blades cut the water as a knife, the ship sails right on laughing at every skipping wave.

There are things now that will happen, which should have happened earlier, if there had been a full response to that first word of the Lord. He might be thinking, 'How things might have been so different?' There are even better things awaiting all as the response is made. That left and lost must be taken and found. The Voice comes as button to buttonhole, and as the two meet there is a drawing together in the cold of the climate. We all have to go back to the place of the original call even as Peter did in John 21:1 to the Lake of Tiberias. He makes sure we are sure, for He is our surety. He pleads until we take up the gift again. We go again and again, until we accomplish something. God had to get the wrong spirit out of Jonah, to get a love into him for the Gentiles.

Part of the second time is the working of God upon the vessel, seeking to mould it to certain perfection, the perfection of the obedient heart. When second opportunity knocks there must be that rocking us out of our complacency. The man who is playing the leading part must be on the stage when the stage is ready and the curtain is raised as a prelude to the 'roof being raised'. When the Lord opens wide, He opens as wide as the world. The door or the mouth opening is just a reflective shadow of the greater things that God opens. Didn't He open and shut the mouth of a Leviathan? The Almighty deals in wind, whale and ocean concepts.

After more training he returns to the battle

After the soldier has received more training he will return into the battle that he withdrew from. He is back there with wounds healed and weapons restored. He has been taken and has looked upon the face of his king. This has granted him fresh inspiration to be a winner and never a loser. While lying injured the King has been to visit him, and he has whispered a few new words into his ear. These have meant so much, as much as rays of sunshine on a cold, frosty morning after a wild midnight storm.

God makes a place in the steps of the one seen afar off, yes the steps of the Lord. What have been Jonah's goings and coming, now become

God's. The voice that created the worlds now speaks a second time to the crumbling clay. His heart has been enlarged to include the Word of Jehovah. Some space has been cleared in the heart for that Word to abide. When it is enthroned then all things work together for good. It is the Word that brings to the place of second activity. It goes as plough blade before the seed can be sown from the hand.

There are opportunities that are wasted

There are wasted waters, a whole ocean of them that have passed under the bridge since that first call. As God remains the same, so do the gifts of His nature. They are given without repentance. There is a whole area of dedication still needing to be taken and used. Use what Destiny has given you just as you would use God to help and direct you. The assuring thing is that Providence keeps us afloat until the second opportunity arrives. As in the old cowboy films we must await until the cavalry comes up from behind to rescue us. God keeps His foot in many a door waiting for us to come to that door from off the floor.

Twice in John chapter one in the Gospel record, John the Baptist had to tell his disciples to look at the Lamb of God that takes away the sins of the world.[1] The secret sometimes is in the second appeal, the second look, and the second prayer. There in John 21: the distant relative of the son of Jonas, Peter has to be commissioned. Twice, young John Mark, the assistant of both the apostle Paul and Silas has to be spoken to before he makes anything for the Master, and before God makes anything of him. During the second day of creation God dealt with the soil that we are made out of in Genesis chapter 1. Light had to be created and received first.[2] Some things are better when they are sent through the water and the fire for a second time. Some glazing takes many times of re-introduction into the flames, and into the hottest part of them. God has done some digging in history to get men to take up their endowment, using it for Him. You will not melt copper until certain degrees of heat are reached, then you can pour it like water into a mould. When He speaks twice we find the second time that the Voice seems mellow. There is something of softness in it. There is a gentleness that was not there when we were first spoken to. It isn't the Voice or the Word that has changed. It is you who have been altered. There has been that drawing into line of the life. It is the gentleness we have responded to gently settled into the mould of His mind. Like David, 'His gentleness has made me great.'[3]

Some changes have to be made

God has to make us into all ears before He can make us into a mouth to speak for him. The last thing He deals with is the mouth and what we have to say. The feet that have turned out of the way, and the hands hanging down must be taken and disciplined, then the rest will come into its proper order at the proper time. Each part of us is a 'proper gift.' The parent of each is obedience. The Word of the Supreme always knows where to find us. How the word came to Jonah we are not told. The Targum says it was in a prophecy.[4] Delivered by an unknown person who is not named. The gifts of the Holy Spirit compliment our gifts. They can and are used to confirm and correct. If they edify us making us strong enough to give our talent back to God, for the glory of the Majesty. Even the shepherd requires the strength to lift and carry the sheep on his back into the pasture from where it strayed.

In each second word there was ointment for the heart

Each word uttered carried ointment to his heart and gave him a new start. This word heard and received in obedience will bring us to trhe place of peace and fulfilment in fruitfulness. There are healing virtues in the words God speaks. 'Speak the word only.' The centurian said in Matthew 8:8. Even those things so long buried that they smell are raised to new life by Divine life. The sacred is lifted back into the sacred. The sun is put back into a black sky. The star, that diamond of the night has its twinkle again. He gave that back to the Giver without going back but by going forward and ever onward. We do this by performing His will. It must be as music coming from the instrument of the heart. The melodies and songs must be sure. Would the appeal work this time? What could be more compelling than Deity speaking to you? His voice goes deeper than food and that digested.

Jonah along with all of us has to love that second word so much that he can't get it out of his mind. All you require is in the Word given. It can open as it can shut. It can heal as it can hurt. It has self-contained elements. There are properties in it of jewel nature.

What did the second opportunity contain?

The Word contained 'the preaching that I bid you.'[5] As if God was saying, 'When you tell them what I say, I will give you more to say.' Obedience is followed by revelation. Obedience is better than sacrifice, obedience is sacrifice. It was to be what he had said and that alone. There must not be the mixing of water with wine resulting in a diluting effect. What he had to say to the people was contained in what God had said to him. Preaching should always be a life being poured out. This is not simply preaching in words, but in deeds and helpful acceptance. "Say My sayings, do My doings, and act My acts". This is the way in which benefits given are fully taken and used. Become an echo of God. That is to be a real talent!

Preach, do and say what I have told you. This not only applies to preaching but to whatever talent we hold. "The word came 'saying'."[6] It describes the blowing of the trumpet in Zion. The word contained in the preaching is described in the call of the shepherd to his sheep. Sometimes it is to warn. Then it is to comfort. It can be just to assure them of his presence. The same word 'saying' is used of Joseph crying when his brethren appeared in his presence.[7] There should be some weeping in Jonah's preaching. He says it through the tears that Jesus wept. What God says in one word is more than all that said from all the pulpits of all ages. It is a Word of variety, and it contains as many wonderful things as the colours in Joseph's coat of many colours.[8] It is multicoloured with such diversity.

God allows things to remind us of our second opportunity

Reece Howells tells in his book on prayer how when as a child he stole some apples. Every apple he saw seemed to shout at him, 'Stop, thief!'. It might have been his conscience shouting at him as the echo of the voice of God. Even the conscience will be what it was created to be. Everytime both Peter and Jonah saw fish, I am sure there would be some message coming from them. When those who are surrendered minister, it sometimes nearly bursts their hearts. Surroundings and happenings have a voice and a message all of their own. God speaks through them.

The response to that second opportunity

It says of the actions in response to the second opportunity that he 'came', 'go', 'arose' 'went', verses Jonah 3:3,4. This speaks volumes of how much he had been prepared and was ready to do what he was told to do. It was responding to the voice that calls us to walk on water. 'I will come if you bid me.'[9] He sped on with the shout of Sovereignty behind him, before him, and to every side of his endeavour. Paul told young Timothy to 'stir up the gift of God.'[10] Fan it into a flame. Rekindle the reason for living. Make it what it was meant to be. Use it and it will use you. Flow with it and it will flow through you. There are so many wedges of gold wrapped in the silk of what a man is. The time has come for the pauper to spend riches provided by another. There is something more stirring in the Word than any spoon stirring even if it is silver or gold. Here are the stirrings as the eagle stirring up its nest to get the eaglets to fly high and low, to use mountaintops as diving boards.

The Word of God rakes out the ashes of dead memories

There is nothing quite like the word of God to rake out the ashes of a sacrifice given long ago. It turns evidence into fact. The ashes must go to allow real fire to live. There can be no sacrifice while those ashes remain. God can do great things through the ashes of a life wasted. He comes as a soft wind to the smoking flax. Alexander Maclaren stood on London Bridge, as a young man and simply kept shouting 'No other Name! No other Name!' Many were converted just through this one act and word. A talent had been taken and used. A man was in an art gallery looking at a picture of Christ on the cross, and he began to say as tears streamed down his face 'And I do love Him, and I do love Him.' Immediately others standing in the crowd around the picture began to say the same. 'We love Him too!' You use what you are and you will encourage others to be true to themselves and their Lord.

Musicians require some note to pitch their instruments to. You might be that musician, you might be the note, and you could be the instrument. Use what you have and are, where it will count the most. Don't be used as a penny when the real value should be a pound. Jonah tried to narrow the largeness of God's nature to the narrowness of his own spirit. The only wooden rule Deity knows is that of the cross of his Son.

There were specific directions to the field of labour. He was not left on some desert Island as marooned, as the moon on a cloudy night. Noah was called into the ark. Annanias was sent to a street called Straight. It was to an old city. That from a past vision re-appeared. The Latin proverb states with authority 'Repetition is the Mother of Studies.' By the repetition and the calling, there is that sinking into the heart, it is slow but as it mills it grinds. Israel was told to lay the commands of God upon their hearts. So that when the heart was broken the commands and word might fall in. The Portuguese tell us that hell is paved with good intentions and roofed with lost opportunities. On the backside of the pattern of hurt and misunderstanding you will see the face of God. From the front it is only a word spoken by somebody not important. Thomas A'Kempis recorded 'God often gives one brief moment that for a long time he has denied.' It is always harder to do the will of God later. Water turns into ice. Molten metal sets. Leaves fall from trees.

The second opportunity means double responsibilities

If Jehovah has granted you a gift, and he has told you twice to use it, that means it is a double-headed gift. Some of the promises and parables of Jesus are prefixed with a double 'verily, verily' as a double challenge. You have a double responsibility. You are going to be doubly used by the Sender. God does not mix, mince or waste His words. When He calls, then He grants the opportunity to respond. The very place in which that has been buried, becomes the commencement of its operation. As you dig deep to unearth that given, you will find that there is still a hand clinging to it, it is the hand of God that will not let go what has been given. He is as devoted to you as that. The same Hand is clasped around you, guiding and helping you to restore the years that the locust and cancer worm has eaten away. Like the rod that Moses used, it flowered again even after it had been cut off.[11] Talents are not found or polished by constant moving around. He had to go back to the beginning of his call. From that same place he caught fresh inspiration as he had witnessed the sails catching wind as they journeyed on the ship. The gift is most used by application where we are. The axe or the electric saw that moves from tree to tree before it has felled one, never cuts down any tree. It just leaves a few marks but never makes its mark. Nothing is more frustrating than going for the help of ointment for healing, to find it is not there. That which can't be trusted is soon rusted. God never said go, and then left you going nowhere, somewhere and everywhere. Even in the act of creation He said let dry land appear. One of the first talents found and formed were in a man called Adam. Let the sun and moon appear as the talents of the sky. They all appeared as he commanded them to be.

Your obedience is part of the second opportunity

Anything apart from 'that great city' would have been a million miles outside of the will of God. Noah must build an ark, as Peter must feed my sheep. The call of God is not open-ended, it is to a specific task. God has not granted you enabling to sit and make daisy chains. Gifts are not toys for boys or dolls for girls, they are weapons to be used to tear down the Strongholds of Darkness. These are not medals given when on holiday, medals come from battles won or lost. The eye cries tears and that is what it was created for. What were you created for? What is your function in life? In the Promise Bible, the book of Ezekiel opens with the words, 'I am Ezekiel', Ezekiel 1:1.

He is called to speak. There must be great preparation, the size of a whale. The only difference between the first opportunity and the second is the word 'second'. It is the second shot that brings the bird to the ground. It is the second whimper that brings a ready response from the mother to the child of her heart. He has to 'cry against it' as some war machine seeking to tear down its walls.[12] Jonah 1:1, the first time he had to, 'cry against it,' the second time; Jonah 3:2, he had to preach 'to it'. As the Word came to him, he has to let that same Word go to them. Let it sit at their feet, and they will sit at its feet. The first time that word came it is recorded that 'he arose and fled.'[13] The second time the difference is 'he arose and went.'[14] He put on the servant's sandals. There is a certain obedience and willingness here. Girded with truth he goes. After we have repented we can expect others to repent. They will become what you are. They will enter into your heart, and take part of that heart unto themselves. God has His way when His word is received and we understand that received in the heart. It is an extended heart through an extended word. As grace is extended to him, he extends it to others. He wasn't now a trumpet with an uncertain sound or a saint with an uncertain future. When the Spanish Armada was sighted in the history of the wars between England and Spain, it took two hours to travel from London to

York in England. The news went on horseback it was conveyed by fires being lit in prominent places, and obedience must be a dash to obey.

Stop being a listener and taster

One Pastor said to his flock 'I want you to stop being 'listeners' and I want you to become 'doers' of the Word. Stop being 'tasters' and start being 'eaters.' The *Message Bible* in Hebrews 5:11, records 'I have a lot more to say about this, but it is hard to get it across to you since you picked up the bad habit of not listening.' When His Word is listened to and received, it tastes like real food, but if it is ignored it is as the crusts cut off the slice of bread for the little children, but we are not children! The old Methodist preacher said 'Procrastination is the death of all things'. Putting it off chokes the life out of every opportunity. Putting it off results in being like the ice bound ship found floating among the icebergs. The captain and the crew were all there with their unfinished meals. They had frozen to death while the ship kept sailing on.

The command was to go to Nineveh

The command was to Nineveh, probably established by Nimrod who 'became a mighty hunter before the Lord.'[15] He was being sent along that same path of duty before the Lord. Some seem to suggest that the word Nineveh is from a root word meaning 'clear waters.' In the Scriptures it is defined as 'a pool of water.' They are not sullied or filled with debris or mud when we obey the God of the servant.

Jonah 3:3, we have a lovely picture of response and repose. 'According to the word of the Lord.' Acting as a branch from the tree trunk. He is as the branch in the Vine. All the sap qualities are flowing through him. He is not only ready to go and have a go, but he has been made ready to go.

Notes

1	John 1:29,36	5	Jonah 3:2	11	Numbers 17:8
2	Genesis 1:1-3	6	Jonah 3:1	12	Jonah 1:2
3	2 Samuel 22:36	7	Genesis 45:2	13	Jonah 1:3
4	The Targum, the Jewish	8	Genesis 37:3	14	Jonah 3:3
	Commentary on the Old	9	Matthew 14:28	15	Genesis 10:8
	Testament	10	2 Timothy 1:6		

CHAPTER 18

The talent compared and contrasted

It is unfair and unnatural to compare unlike with like. There is carnality about comparing success with success, or lack of success. If we are on a level playing field then all is well. Sometimes we compare one thing with another when and where there is no comparison at all. All men are not made equal but some are more equal than others. Thumb and finger comparison is dangerous. It is unfair to the point of being bilious when comparing one with something quite different. There are chalk and cheese equations in God. The plank of wood must never be likened to the sailing ship or the oar for rowing with a toothpick. It can become a two-horse race when we begin to compare one thing with another, jealousy entering the race at some stage. Comparison will always fall at the first hurdle. The river must not be equalled to the sea and the pond must not be likened unto the lake. This must never be stated that more boats sail on the sea than on the river or the pond, for that is unjust. There mustn't be the placing of success alongside of success, particularly if one has had far more opportunities. The one hand holds many talents while the other has only the fingers on the hand. One can be an empty hand while the other is full. The first might be empty because it has given everything. The other is full because it belongs to a miserly spirited person. When we compare one talent with another, we are trying to find points of agreement and disagreement. In that contrast, we set one in opposition to the other. We do this in order to show superiority. One stands in opposition to the other, never working together for the mutual good of both.

He had the greater talent

All I have said is true, but in this small book of Jonah all that is written is reversed. It is Jonah with his multitude talented life. The truth is stranger than that for it is fiction. The very opposite is the truth. The small becomes the great, and the great becomes less than the small. It is good for us to compare scripture with scripture, and see how much blessing the created contains. When we look at the heart of Jonah, he is the worm, as it gnaws away the tree, and you will see it has a greater appetite for that challenge before it, than Jonah ever had. It never runs away. The work is here and it completes it.

The secret of your success is not your talent

The secret of what takes place is found and founded in the facts of this epistle of Jonah. The word 'Lord' is found twenty six times in these pages. The sovereignty of God is stamped all over every happening, sometimes seen and heard, but at other times neither seen or heard. The word used for Lord is Jehovah, the self-existing God. The 'I Am' which is almost untranslatable. It means 'I will be what I will be.' Make that your copy and you will never 'blot your copy book.' He is the covenant keeping Jehovah. You do your work and allow Him to do His. Your talent will be used greatly by God. I will be what God has made me to be, even if that means being a worm. There is such a contrast here, and you would readily think that Jonah should come out as the winner resplendent in the glory of what happened. The answer is the reversal. One goes heavenward while the other is buried in the earth. The secret of all achievement is centred in the crown of his head. Make Him ordinary, and you will become ordinary. As you regard Him, as you love Him, you love others as brothers. One, Jonah, sleeps in the sun, while the worm works willingly.

God prepares his instruments

There is a succession of instruments prepared by God and used by Him to establish His will. If you put the son of the prophet into the class - he wears the dunces cap. He is at the bottom of everything. His response is slow and weak. Those of another nature, a wild beast nature readily conform to God's moulding, squeezing hand. The great fish, the wind, the sea, the gourd and a worm are all part of His tools of the trade of getting men to use what has been left with them until He returns. God has an army of creatures ready and willing to obey Him. He chooses those who have a choice, and then that army is used to illustrate how we should respond even in our darkest moments. It is comparatively easy for the butterfly to fly in the sun, but can it, will it do it, in the wind and the rain? Even the clouds are depicted as His chariots with lightening as His many spears of the years.

Always behind the scenes God is at work, preparing us just as He prepared the wind and the whale, for our final destiny. There is a touch here and there. He knows why He allows so many things, which are part of a moulding process. Some happenings are meant to raise the talent from the earthly things they are buried in. We can and do look at a worm and a man and declare with some assurance and inspiration that the worm is the winner by a large measure. It had an appetite for success. The worm will be declared the winner.

The wonder of a willing worm

The worm in the Scriptures is an emblem of human weakness.[1] When we add to it the Lordship of Sovereignty then we have a thoroughbred winner. It is so because even in the weakness of a worm you can find strength to obey. It never presumes on grace or God's forgiveness. It seeks no crown to wear, only a work to be fully accomplished. Aesop's fable of 'The Tortoise and the Hare' ably illustrate what happened with Jonah and the worm. The slowest won the race. It was slow in movement but quick in response. The race wasn't won by the most talented. This was not Jonah and the whale. Even in that, this man would be the loser by a large chunk of fish. What talent the worm had was fully used and developed. It ate its way into the will of Jehovah. In it were all the seeds for accomplishment. It used all of its body, soul and spirit to devour the Palm Christ.*

The glory of the growing gourd

The Cambridge Bible for Schools declares that the 'gourd' is called the 'Palm Christ' because its leaves portray an outstretched hand resembling the hand of Jesus stretched out on the cross.[2] The worm crawled its way into the challenge, and after disappearing for a while arose again as if from the dead, as a conqueror. Whatever it was best at - that was its talent. It wanted to use its might, the might of a maggot for its Maker. It couldn't preach or sail ships, but it could worm its way in.

It threw itself with its talent into its work. Unlike the other worker it did not run away and go to play. It went for that gourd as something

* This is the name given to the Juniper tree, and it is known by this name.

hungry to be a winner. Without an axe or saw, pick or shovel, it toppled the tree as a hurdle before it. It cleared the ground for new growth.

God sometimes becomes to us what we are. As a fish to a fish and as man to men. He became a worm to this prophet. It could rise early and begin at the bottom. It was like King David who felled Goliath. Here was a 'Palm Christ' full of oil that needed to be felled. Who would have such an appetite for the Master's will as to eat that full of oil? It was not a success and its talents were not fully deployed, until that before it fell at its feet harnessed by the law of gravity. That was given back to the Sender in small-conquered portions. Big things were brought down to its own size. It accomplished it little by little, not all at once with a mighty shout. The acclamation for the work it did wasn't heard in the blowing of a trumpet. It was in the quiet application of what it was and had to the task it had undertaken by Divine orders. It couldn't have been more devoted if it had been an aeroplane or some other war machine. Whatever it found to do - it did it with all its might. This is a glowing report when compared with the dead letter that reports all Jonah was called to do but didn't do. The shining and the supremacy of a talent are not its nature but how it is put to use. If it is put to good use it will put others to the shame of the blushing cheek and the burning conscience, being the initial evidence of all such happenings.

Only a worm but it used its talent

Where this worm was born, in what handful of soil it existed in, we will never know. How it could, as part of its mission fill itself with castor oil, the greatest prophet cannot prophecy. The plant died because this worm did its work. The worm lives on in this story. It had a talent for smiting things.

Four times the word 'prepared' appears in the story of 'contrasting talents',[3] and in another tense it is translated 'appointed',[4] you could write on all its wrinkles 'By Royal Appointment to His Majesty.' God used dirt to prepare it. In the caverns of the soil, there it was raised and trained. The very darkness that surrounded it put something of lasting value into it. That entered into it that could be used by God. This miner became a carpenter as it felled the plant.

With dim sight it saw what to do

Worms have very good hearing but very poor sight. Possessing sight like this thing helped it to have only one vision. If only we could say what Mary James wrote, 'Since my eyes were fixed on Jesus, I've lost sight of all besides; so enchained my spirit's vision looking at the crucified.' Its eyes and mind were focused on the Palm Christ. It can hear very well and it reminds us of Him of whom it is written 'My ear have you digged.'[5] The Hebrew love slave would have his ears bored with an awl to the doorpost of his master's house.[6] It commenced work at the first call and not at the last. It didn't just get in by the skin of its existence. It commenced at the bottom to work its way to the top. How different from the sent one who wanted to be at the forefront all the time except when he was asleep! Sometimes it is not what the World or Church designate as great talents that really count. What all the other prepared things failed to accomplish this worm of a thing carried it out and sent the man of mission on his way. It depends what you need how you define it. A person suffering from a fatal disease will tell you that penicillin was a great discovery. It was required and requested by him and it healed him. That same person may not feel the same way about the invention of the humble humbug. That tree of oil was a Goliath and the worm had to bring it down. When it felled it, just as the Greeks believe and be taught. When you destroyed an enemy the strength of the one overcome was supposed to enter you. In the next conflict you faced, you had the added strength from the previous encounter and victory. There was another strength aiding you. This oil bottle must be broken. It was felled without the dynamite of the Prophet's Office.

God uses the small things of this world

God uses the faith of a child. A few fish that are the makings of a miracle are a young lad's lunch.[7] A small nail is used in the Book of Judges for accomplishment in the hands of a woman.[8] Dorcas with her needle, these are small talents that are so useable and useful.[9] Jesus used a coin taken from a fish's mouth and preached a sermon about it.[10] From one spark there can emerge a thousand flames. That which wouldn't heat a finger can be so multiplied as to heat a whole hospital. The word 'worm' is a good description of the little finger. The small act or deed as found in the New Covenant word 'helps'.[11]

A worm can change the colour of things

The word used to describe the heart and soul of this worm is that from where we obtain dye. It could change the colour of things and it did. There was nothing left the same where the worm came. That left by the man, Jonah was just the same when he left as when he came. There was nothing different. There were no fallen trees in his garden to make pulpits from. No oil factory was established. It is this worm that the prophet Isaiah refers to when he says 'Though your sins be as red like 'crimson' they shall be as white as wool.' The margin of Jonah 4:10 (King James Version) speaks of the gourd as a 'son of the night' needing to be destroyed by that having received light. Every talent is given not for self-illumination or gratification but to destroy the works of the night. There must be no in-breeding in us or in the worm.

This worm does not exist for itself but for another. It is there as you are to establish another Kingdom not based on ships and going to sea. Here was a worm of a thing that could climb trees because it had learned to obey the prompting of God. I wonder how many books you have read or how many sermons you have heard based on the talents of the worm? That heard, understood and read could be measured by worm measurements! Miracles are always connected to great prophets such as Elijah and Elisha. Here is a book of miracles written on a small-scale scroll. What Elohim did when he brought all the animals in creation to Noah's ark, he did in bringing this worm to work for Him? When you compare this worker with Jonah, size for size; and gift for gift, the comparison is unbearable. It should have been 'a walk over' for the man sent to Nineveh. Of His fullness we have all received gift for gift.

The greatest talent is that used by you

The greatest gift is that used by you. The most talented people in the universe are those dedicated to the work of God. You might feel like a real worm. You are tired of standing and holding the ladders while others ascend them into fame. This means that you have a strong arm and hand, and Providence is using it. Somebody must stand and open the door for the successful. This is what this worm was doing. Jonah becomes the worm and the worm becomes the man. The prophet has become the companion of worms even before his death. It topples the plant but in doing so it is sowing seeds of encouragement. What talent Barnabas had, the son of consolation. Those who encourage others to do great things, are made great themselves in the greatness they encourage in others. This after growth is harvested by all, reaping a rich and full harvest from its field of activity.

The important thing is your character

The miracles of the book of Jonah on a small scale are not important. It is the character and the gifting of the man. What he builds for others, as an example, is the important achievement. Character and not charter will decide what we do with that deposited in human clay. Character is far more important than gift. As the finger is more important than the ring it holds. It is the best, the 'more excellent way' when we have character and gifting together.[12]   Very few things are then thrown overboard and very few ships sink. It is strange how the name Jonah has become synonymous with bad happenings. While worms become food to keep birds in flight. God is developing you for the future. The future becomes more important than the present.   Character is far more important than the tools of the trade. The oak cabinet is far more admired and required than the tools that fashioned it. The worm works while the man sleeps. There is a sound of gnawing from this grub while there is the sound of snoring from the chosen one. The call of God is demonstrated fully in a felled tree or plant. Some go on holiday in the sun while the short tube stays until its work is completed. It could say, 'I have finished the work you gave me to do'. The fallen gourd was evidence enough of a talent fully used.

The Creator working with small things can do many things. Working with that contained in the Hebrew prophet He has difficulty with. In that surrendered the sender establishes his workshop. Never think that He only works with oceans and whales. He uses the sun, moon and twinkling stars. He works with rods and the jawbone of any ass.

It is not the size of the gift, large or small, but the sheer devotion of the possessor of that given. It is attitude and direction counting as large things in this Kingdom. It isn't built on walls or foundations as such but on sacrifices, attitudes, sheer determination and that done in the name of Jehovah. It had something to go to and cling to. It didn't stay to pity or embrace itself or drown itself in a pool of pity or petty. Saying, 'I am so small and I can't achieve much.' There was no use for it to think of its smallness or weakness. It was part of that army such as Fanny Crosby, Helen Keller and Marylyn Baker who got on with using whatever they had. They might have been placed in the shade, but from that shade they have put sunshine into others. Using their darkness they have created diamonds of light and lustre.

Use what you have and be used

Dr Strong in his Hebrew lexicon says part of the root word from where the word 'worm' comes from, means 'to keep blurting out' as if when it feeds it keeps sending food out. It is suggesting to keep speaking. If only we could be as hungry for God as this worm was for the leaves of the Juniper tree! It had weak power, but it applied all its weakness and defeated a greater power than itself. Only a worm but it became larger than a tree. A few inches in the ground but it toppled something up in the sky. Unlike the wayward one not willing to use his mouth. This worm used all the axes set in its gums by Jah.* Keep blurting it out. Keep saying it until you believe it. Talk about it until you do it. Talk before you leap. This small invertebrate ploughed fields and gardens yet it was used to chop a tree down. Here is the wisdom of the wise. It was called to destroy the only living thing in a desert. There was the breaking of conventional things and lying them low before the Supreme.

A worm can do more than a lion

A living worm is better than a dead lion. A living worm is better than a dead eagle. A living, eating, chewing, small thing is better than a herd of dead elephants. The whale was dead. The boat had sailed to another port. The captain and crew had disembarked. One with a small gifting doing the work of Adonai is far better than one who is called a 'one man band.' No music came from the sleeper, but plenty came from the eater. God did not expect it to fly like a bird or swim like a fish. It had to do what it was created to do - no more and no less. It couldn't be a hammer to knock nails into wood. It was the Gideon of the Worm Army.[13] If you have no public ministry then do it privately. Be part of God's Private Army.

* Jah , the shortened name of Jehovah. When the Israelite didn't want to pronounce the full name of Jehovah he would use this shortform.

There, where Jonah failed it did its best work. When some falter and fail to use what God has given us doing our most successful work.

It saw the tree right through. Success in this story was eating and feasting while he was sleeping. Doing the will of God was like eating at a royal banquet. It made castor oil the flavour of the month. Many with eyes half shut during a yawn will ask you how did you find time? We must redeem the time. We have to buy it back from the world and not surrender it as this mad mouse did in the shape of a man. Between the breaths taken in, it had time for a few more chews of wood. There are many saying today 'Where is the Lord God of Elijah?' God is answering with a question of his own 'Where are the Elijahs?' In trying, too many people stop trying. Don't get too discouraged, it might be that the last key on the ring which fits the lock.

John Calvin states in his commentary on the book of Jonah 'Since God, then, is reconcilable, if the Ninevites will return to the right way and flee to Him, He will instantly embrace them: thus I shall be found false in my preaching.'

This small mole of the soil could have been sent some assistant but it did what it had to do alone. God could have sent that raging storm from the sea and uprooted it. The whale, with one mighty gulp, would have swallowed both Juniper tree and the worm. That isn't how God performs His plans.

There will always be a second opportunity for all

There is always an opportunity for the small to flourish in God. The large goes smaller while the small grows larger. If diet is Deity and doing His will, this will lead to God-growth. This appetite feeds on it, as one might have bacon and eggs for breakfast. It could never grow into a dragon until it had learned to be a worm. Jonah will never be a greater man until he discovers some manly qualities in himself. There are whole regions in his life, that lie as that never discovered. There is still much that is virgin in the kingdom. There is an upper room where the wind of Pentecost has never filled and blown. There is no other use until he is all used up for the Maker.

The worm did what it could

It is doing what it can do best in boring holes. As it bores it strikes oil. It becomes a woodworm, then in it a bookworm because it has its name recorded in Holy Writ, but it must become both a glow-worm and a silkworm. There is such a need for this small capacity to worm its way in and show the greater and the more talented what can be done if we give it all to the Creator. It used the tree to crawl to its Maker. As it worked and applied what it had, it came nearer to God. It didn't judge its success by its size. There was no counting of leaves, roots or stems so that others might be impressed with its accomplishments.

There is something so deeply fulfilling in using what you have for God. The candle must shine and as it shines so it shares. It might be losing its life but it is showing the way to others who are noble. Those other people are able to light greater lamps such as lighthouses and arch lights. Paul refers to the Philippian believers as his joy and crown.[14] Nothing can be more rewarding than that. It became God's tree chopper but not helicopter. The snail can never run with the hares and the hounds but it can remove that hindering them. Is Jonah listening to all this? If you see what seems to be a hole in the ground and you wriggle into it, it is the will of the One sending you. It is in that very hole that self-life is buried forever. It is here we die, as the small tool that was lost in the tree. After England went to war with the Argentineans on the Falkland Islands, the soldiers were presented to the Queen; when she commented on the bravery of one man he replied 'It was only part of the training.'

Dedication does bring in a new colour

The worm was about to change the whole contour and colour of Jonah's thinking. In its dedication it added much colour – the manifold grace of God – to the story recorded. When I say colour, I mean a new concept and dimension. The story had finished. Everything was about to disappear until the worm came as a pen to add an addendum by what it accomplished. All in the life of the prophet has been clerical grey so far. It takes this little finger to bring new colour into the story. Talent used can add other colours to your life such as the pink of joy and the blue of contentment. Cloths and silks used to be dyed with the colour received from it. That fit for a peasant to wear was turned into the coronation gown of a king. It meant it had to die, as we all do if there is to be any accomplishment. If men are going to sing songs about us then we must do something worth singing about. National songs are based on great wars and battles won. Let the small gifting become the real artist that changes finger painting of pre-school days into real art. There can be new shades and the deepening of what is already there. Mix your own sweat and tears with the paint.

That cloth on the Communion Table needn't be the same old white week after week. Surrender what you have and God will put some colours, many different colours into your week. The colours in the Greek word for 'manifold' mean many colours will be added to life.[15] The worst colour in the world is the religious colour that Jonah wore in his heart. It is so boringly the same. This needs faith the size of this creature to change all that. It is from the word given here as 'worm' that we obtain the word 'scarlet' when the scarlet thread that the prostitute of Jericho, Rahab placed in the window for deliverance. A worm, or many worms, had to die to produce that. Here is the message for the person who feels they are like this snail without a shell in their limited ministry.

You can change society by your service

As salt we preserve society. As light we illuminate society. As small influences we can change the colour of society and how people think and react to one another. There is only one way to be fulfilled in the Christian Life, and that is not whether you feel that your enrichment is large or small. It is to have a great hunger for God, as voracious as this little worm had for the castor oil plant. In its hunger it didn't wait for its favourite food but what God said. The plant was bigger than this slitherer but not bigger than its appetite. Hunger will make you big enough to swallow castor oil in doses the size of a tree.

If you had to write a book to tell all the stories of your conquests would they just fill a thimble? A famous man arranged to meet with an evangelist of the last century called D. L. Moody. As soon as he met him he told Mr Moody that he had been converted fourteen years. The evangelist immediately asked him 'What have you done since?' This worm was willing to go on its belly for God. How different from the serpent in the Garden of Eden! There is an old saying 'To have a worm in your tongue.' It means to tell everything. To have so much to tell that you are uneasy until it is said. To have something to say and it moves and squirms until you have said it. It suggests to keep barking like a dog and refusing to keep quiet about the matter. What a picture of sheer and sure devotion to its Maker and Feeder! The one who should have been saying things is strangely silent on all fronts. He only speaks to complain.

God will give praise for work well done

All will stand before God and appear before the Bema Seat* of Jesus Christ.[16] Many will appear and tell great stories of their exploits. Finally, just before the books are closed this worm appears and is asked what it accomplished in life and it will say 'I felled a gourd for God.' 'Well done you great and faithful servant!' It was through a worm that Jehovah brought the final rebuke to the soul of the prophet. He is saying 'before you complain look at the exploits of the little grub. See what it did, how great it all is when compared with you and your many gifts. I gave it no ship or whale yet it fully obeyed me. Go and look at the ants and the conies you sluggard but you can become a worm.' A worm on the page of God's Book. Two will stand before the Sovereign - the worm and the prophet. Yes, in that precise order of merit and accomplishments. There were many little twisting things in the heart of this man. When compared with the small he is not tall. The thing of substance is in this small matter. This fishes meal has grown taller in the work it has done. It has grown tree tall, while the prophet has diminished to the size of a wishbone. The worm threw all it had at the tree until all was accomplished. May the wise read and understand, and where ignorance is bliss it is folly to be wise.

* Bema Seat (Greek) – a raised platform to which athletes came to receive their laurels for competing in Grecian games. See Vine's Expository Dictionary of Biblical Words, 1985 edn p337.

Notes

1	Job 17:14.25:6. Psalm 22:6	5	Psalm 40:6	12	1 Corinthians 13:1-3
		6	Exodus 21:6	13	Judges 6.7.8.
2	The original Cambridge Bible for Schools and Colleges	7	Matthew 14:17	14	Philippians 4:1
		8	Judges 4:21-26	15	1 Peter 1:6. 4:10
		9	Acts 9:39	16	Romans 14:10
3	Jonah 1:4,17.4:6,7	10	Matthew 17:27		
4	Daniel 1:5,10	11	1 Corinthians 12:28		

CHAPTER 19

The consecrated talent

It produces an abundant harvest when the seed is sown and dies and all is dedicated to the glory of Majesty. When what we give comes from that source and we give it back to that source, that is dedication. When the Knights of the Round Table gathered with King Arthur, he said whoever made a conquest could wear the crown on the table. They entered the palace on returning, and one of them, taking the crown he could have legitimately worn, placed it back on the king's head. It adds glory to glory when we seek not our own. As found in Philippians 2. Jesus didn't grasp at what could have been His.

Consecration will always bring success

When Jonah was concerned enough to travel into Nineveh, then there were tremendous results brought about by his consecration. He gave himself as a living sacrifice to seeing that city repent. One act brought them from off their backs and placed them on their knees. Instead of saying prayers they prayed them. In place of ritual there was reality. One talent led the way as some choirmaster. Truth was no longer bent into circles by their blacksmiths as they pleased. We can have many talents but until they are offered upon the Altar of Free Will, they will only go up from that altar as smoke rather than the smell of a well pleasing sacrifice. I don't want whatever we have that is as small as a thimble, or as large as some tower block to conclude as dust and ashes. I want it to be fully used by God.

God uses our devotion to establish His Kingdom on earth. Work for God always continues throughout all generations. It takes but a small decision to accomplish something for ever. There has to be the formation of something of value while we are here and in the now. There has to be the avoidance as much as avoiding nuclear fall-out or some mysterious plague simply leaving footprints in the sand of time. Any old wind will blow across them obliterating them forever. With a pen of iron and that of laser-beam quality the talent can make its mark for time and truth going towards eternity. It entered into the homes, the palace, the fields and commerce even into the pigsty of the day. Surrender is one of the most beautiful words in the Bible and the English Language. It has been given for our learning and admonition.

The speed at which consecration moves us

In Jonah chapter three, the moment Jonah entered swiftly through the doors of Nineveh, the talent was acting as if it had been fully consecrated all the time. That bound and fettered was set free. Way was made for it as a man's gift will make room for him. The results of a revival were seen because a man gave all that presented to him, to the people of his day. He emptied out the full barrel as they did in Elijah's miracle of fire, 1 Kings 18:33. They felt as others have felt, throughout the ages, the impact of that surrender, with all the strings of the parcel cut free and hanging loosely for the receiver to open it right up.

There is surrender in consecration

Every musical instrument must surrender itself in one way or another before any music will sound out. The strings have to be plucked, as a bow must pass over some strings. Others have to be plucked and the drum has to be beaten while the cymbals are really hurt. Jonah had come to the realisation that for you to be really dedicated there is a cost of fame and reputation to be sacrificial. Surrender literally means 'to give it away'.

The meaning of consecration

The word 'consecrate' is a Bible word and attached to it are many other sentences. It means 'to fill the hands'. The hands so full of what Jehovah has given. There is the figure of nothing held back. See a child in youthful innocence take from a sweet jar, and in its blind hunger and zeal, attracted by the glittering wrappers it will take such a handful as not to allow air to travel between the sweets. Jonah's hands that were folded into sleep now become the hands that carry the heart of God tenderly to these needy people. Sleep patterns never produce life role models. This word consecration is the word used when the High priests of the Old Testament were dedicated to God.[1] Part of the offering of that day was placed in the hands of the Priest. It identified him with sacrifice and approach to God. His hands were stained with sacrifice. He never had to have empty hands in the future. There was no place left in those hands to take any other thing for him; it was all taken what was given. If the sacrifice had just been killed then he received a pattern in blood on those arm ends. When Jesus was nailed to a Roman stick of wood, his hands were filled that had never been empty. When the Israelite was counting his sheep to give one in every ten to God, it was the tenth one that was marked as being consecrated. This sheep or lamb was the 'one that had passed under the shepherd's rod.'

When a city was taken, the crown of the king and the gold with cattle were consecrated to God. In fact, the kings, they died – yes, they were killed. They were given to destruction. This is the true meaning of consecration so help me God! They could never be offered or given to anything else. In fact the word became synonymous with the word 'curse.'[2] It was like a thing with a curse upon it and it could not be used or introduced into any other area. This is true consecration when we let God use our talents as Jonah's were used, as he came into the named city.

Consecration is investing what we have

When the prophet entered the city, because he had surrendered what God had invested, the happenings were remarkable. There was repentance and there was accomplishment. The word 'repentance' used for this new approach to the Eternal is very interesting because it is from a root word meaning in modern parlance 'a sharp intake of breath.'[3] It is to take a deep breath and gulp. This suggests taking in fresh air. It suggests we require what God is giving. It takes our breath away when we think of the longsuffering of God. When we believe we are as the Queen of Sheba, who when she had listened to King Solomon, and seen the way in which they all lived there was no more breath in her. When we gaze at the cross, and the empty tomb, there is no more breath in us. Everything God does is 'pause for thought'. When a miracle takes place, such as took place in Nineveh, there is a sharp intake of breath. In the Acts of the Apostles, chapter 2:4, the wind filled the place where they were sitting, and they could breath that which God had sent. In Luke 15, it says that the Prodigal Son 'came to himself' as if he had been short of breath and in a faint. When returning to the father he breathed a sigh of relief. God will grant us 'times of refreshing', fresh, gentle winds, from His presence. When we use that gift there is a pause by people as we minister. They are caused to stop and think. It is the look before they leap. We bring people to a place, making them stop and stare as they breathe deeply. They feel they have to climb stairs and do difficult things so they breathe deeply. How many have been turned into tears as they have listened to great oratory or seen some act of kindness that has turned their hearts into liquid?

Lives were changed all because that held dear was not dearer than the One who was being served. The talent was let go as it was set loose- as he began to preach the preaching and to say the saying he had been told to say. He found to his amazement that it does work if we let it go and let the Maker do a makeover and take over. Any gift will lead the way for others to follow. If I am in the hands of the Eternal! Come with me and we will do you good. That given to the Creator is taken and what is found wanting receives its perfect balance from the character of God and the power of God. If you take out your trumpet, they will take out theirs, and the result will be much trumpet sounding in Zion. The nail can become a mighty sword. When Gideon told his men to break those water jars, the middle had to be broken out of them so the light they contained could shine through, it did and there was a great victory.[4] Sometimes for us to be used and useable, there has to be a breaking point. The vessel means so little and the light shines so greatly. Among the broken pieces there are shining lights. These are the things that happen when normal things are sanctified with sacrifice.

Consecration doesn't change our ability

That talent is harnessed to one purpose as a man with only one eye concentrates the one thing on the one thing. The thought can become a word and a deed. Legs that are short and stubby, unable to move very quickly, begin to move at such great speed that he enters the city on the first day. In the book of Leviticus the slow moving creatures such as the worm and tortoise are considered unclean. The old nag has become a thoroughbred. It is attitude of heart and mind that counts. When it all adds up, it adds up to rarity. When we see it dedicated, it opens the mouth wide to tell, it grants faith to the heart to believe that it is going to bring success. The lean years of the bare boards of the ship are finished with. He has to be as the flag on the rope flying from the mast. How did it reach such dizzy heights? By being handed over and tied to one piece of rope and forgetting the many pieces it might have been made part of.

'This one thing I do', is part of the success story on parade before us. It has been unfurled and totally given to what it has to do. All choice has been removed in the choice that it has made. This preacher knew that the captain of that vessel he had travelled on went from port to port because he was given over to the one ship and not the many. If you stand with one foot on land and one in the sea, you are in the same troubled waters as Jonah ever was. Some of those waters can be poured into your soul. That surrendered brings to us a matter of urgency. Zeal is restored to the feet and every faculty as if some angelic wind has blown upon us. That with seemingly no tongue and only one leg receives the extra impetus for impediment. He runs like a centipede. For the blushing cheek he receives the warm glow of doing what he should have done some days earlier. He is now the early bird that catches the worm. The sent one is pushed not only to the edge. He goes over the edge as he is used to edge his way at snail pace. God can wait.

Consecration comes through preparation

While he is waiting the talent is being developed ready for its moment of glory. If it is crafted enough it will be too precious to bury anywhere. He needed to bury it in the needs of those in the Great City he was sent to, as the artist will bury his paints on the canvas. They appear in another more beautiful form than lumpy paint on the pallet. All that was a gift needed to be given away so that more might be given to him. As we pour out God pours in. In the book of Proverbs it says 'Those that water shall be watered.'[5] That received back will be pressed down, shaken together and running over. It is almost as if the ship has found deep water and it launches forth with such zest. The difference is depth and purpose. These are the things that are by-products of the 'consecrated talent.' He now has something to do. A purpose has enlarged his heart.

The man was held up by an excuse. It does matter that we use what we have graced to us. God has blown upon the smoking flax, and as it enters the city or somewhere there it bursts into flames.[6] There is a conviction in what he says. He isn't talking to the drunken sailors now. The days of looking for a light to kindle a fire under the sacrifice of the heart are over and done with. He treads a sure pathway because he treads an obedient one. Wherever it concludes if he is willing to be used, Jehovah Nissi will be at the end of it to do some flag waving. The steps of a good man are being ordered by the Lord.

Everyone has a talent that needs to be consecrated

When you come to the Dictionary of Talents there are millions written as records on every page? Each one is a token of grace to the Human Race. You have no requirement to turn any page. The first page you come to - your talent is written there. It is not what you thought it was. God is saying, 'already you have the talent for reading, thinking, acting independently, and turning the pages of life'. The gift we are looking for isn't what it seems to be. It is not even what you think it is. The talent never left Jonah even when he ran away. It was buried somewhere. God marks the place with a Cross. It can be the most ordinary thing that you do. If you raise your hand to lift something from a shelf, that is easy and so normal. If you are raising your hand to get something from a shelf to give to another less fortunate than your self that becomes a talent. When you prepare the Communion with those same hands, gifts are at work.

Jonah was doing what he did best and that was to prophesy to the people. Words are always ladders up into the hearts of people. That given is the first step leading to the King's throne. They are let loose from the cage as the Dove of Help was here. Those same hands that are lifted in worship suddenly are holy hands lifted up in prayer. It is as the Almighty sees it and not as we see it. All the man who saw the future had to do was go and say things to these people. That required to be uttered he had known it for many days, but he had never come to the altar with it. He always came with an emptiness of heart. If God had told him to simply preach or sing, blow a trumpet or use a million talents then that is what he should have done. So many times it isn't the things God wants us to do, but the one thing. When we can be trusted with one thing, then we can be trusted with many. Ultimately we have to be trusted with anything. In eternity, God wants to make you ruler over many things, because you were faithful with one. King David was faithful with a few sheep, but he became a ruler of many nations.

Consecration turns the ordinary into a talent

Things that are so ordinary are so talented. Jonah, you son of Jonah stop looking for what you already have! Talents aren't normally sorted out and used as old stamps on envelopes. They are where we need them. The lamp is not looking for its light; it is using it for all to see. A man falls down a hole in the road. It is very deep and dark. He will use all he has to help himself to get back to where he commenced before his fall. His talents, gifting, helps - call them what you will but all come into play in that situation.

When we look at ourselves we 'see through a glass darkly'[7] but when we look at the main character of this Book we see him as face to face. It is as if a mirror has been placed before us and what we see in him is our selves. There are certain things in him we see and admire but we need to burn his weeds and cultivate his flowers. The reason that we admire him is that he could be our twin. He is not the man who lives next door but the person that sits with me everywhere I go. You know the person I have most trouble with. That is here having escaped out of his own heart. Looking at him is the gazing into the photograph album of our family.

Consecration breaks the boring pattern of things

Much of his life is as flat as the proverbial pancake. He dwells on marsh water where nothing grows. There are no foundations built but if you wait around long enough, you will be the very witness of strange happenings. The only time we see real development and growth is when he decides to go to that city of calling and beckoning. It is as if when God says 'go' he interprets that as 'grow'. The word 'grow' is seen in the word 'go'. It is at the precise moment of challenge that the grace given to him begins to 'glow'. The relevant part of his life comes into activity, just as if he has been holding playing cards in the hand, or chess pieces in waiting. He is playing for big stakes. Within that hand of cards, one card is a King. It has the picture of a King upon it. Surely, there comes the moment for him to 'play his cards right'.

It seems as if we have to be placed in circumstances, sometimes adverse ones, before we will allow all those talents to operate. Jonah, like us becomes the reluctant partner. He had been a sleeping partner. That received is used and it touches the King on the throne.

In consecration the real and the true are released

It is true, real consecrated talent does this. It moves people to tears. That done is such a real thing that it has the ring of truth about it. We know we can be doing our work for the Lord God but be on automatic pilot, just going through the ritual, when God demands the real thing. The runaway train keeps going but it has no driver. This engine is moving but it is going nowhere. Those who are going nowhere reach their destination and never know that they have arrived there. Through Jonah's preaching sixty thousand people were saved.[8] Wasn't that worth using his grace gift for? The smooth places make the rough ride worth it all. His gifting was now applied to the things which mattered. If you want a symbol of consecration, use the sun, moon and stars. They constantly give themselves to their orbit without deviation. Watch the bee and the butterfly go from flower to flower until they create something.

When the pilgrim in Pilgrim's Progress came to the hill called 'Difficulty', he had to attempt to climb it three times. He had to go back to the bottom and start again. There was a spring at the bottom, not at the top for refreshment for the weary.[9] Drink again, and think again, before you go on. That around you demands for their sake that you devote your talent. From the moment of letting go of it, new things appear. It was working with the tool that turned a whole nation seeking after God. That with no heart was given a new heart and a new song. Those who were sullen and sullied became seekers after the Almighty.

Through Jonah part of the plan was introduced. When they realised what it was they weren't happy with part of it - they wanted the truth, the whole truth and nothing but the truth.

We lose our appeal when we appear empty handed. Here were people with hands held out wanting help from God. Without a prism the diamond is only glass. It was the sanctifying of that received, bringing the benefits felt by one and all in the nation. If he comes with a fullness, that completed can be shared. If there is devotion in him it can be offered as a relationship with the living God. Whatever he is they are likely to become. The sacrifice is on the altar. Let us see more than smoke or ashes, let us see the real fire, that embraced sent into flames. Let the sacrifice be consumed. May your consuming passion be to serve Him. Love Him, know Him, but serve Him.

What happened here is what happened in one Welsh revival. One man used his talent for reading, and he read from the Anglican Litany, and he reached the words 'By thine agony and bloody sweat, good Lord deliver us.' Many burst into tears weeping aloud and unashamedly as the words were uttered. Moods with emotions and deepest thoughts flooded out in tears of repentance.

Consecration will bring the talent into its ministry

In the Welsh revival a talent had come into its own ministry and heralded a move of God in the Land of Song. A doctor said 'All the debts on my books have been cleared.' Jonah preached and they believed God. He let loose and let go. All that happened in Nineveh followed in the wake of an awakening. He spearheaded that repentance and faith. When the Sovereign managed to get the leading player into his place with all systems working, then it was easy to bless others. Why did it tarry so long? Ask the son of Israel to do the explaining. As the one piece was found and put in place, all the rest fitted into the mosaic. The jawbone of an ass would only ever be a jawbone of an ass until it died. When it was placed in a hand, it became a mighty weapon of war, killing heaps upon heaps, Judges 15:16

Consecration takes us to the right hand of God

When it says 'they believed'[10] it can mean to 'go to the right hand.' It is that hand that grants and forms enrichments to be used for the King. This is the place of power and granting forgiveness. All this saved it from 'perishing', the same word and judgement used of Sodom and Gomorrah. Only God knows how large a key we hold in that deposited within our hearts. It can unlock many doors, throwing away many chains binding the hearts of the people. What you have can be as the Trojan Horse bringing Troy to destruction once it was taken inside the city. We may not lead a city to God but we can lead one to know their Creator. If you can begin with what you have in a small way, that little donkey may take Jesus into Jerusalem to clean out the temple of His father and commence worship afresh in the hearts of people. It only happens when something happens to us. In the yielding is the healing, in the giving is the helping - a talent not buried.

Notes

1	Exodus 29:24	6	Matthew 12:20. See the	9	John Bunyan who wrote
2	Deuteronomy 7:26		author's book 'In		this Christian Allegory
3	Jonah 3		Sickness and in Health'	10	Jonah 3:5
4	Judges 7:19	7	1 Corinthians 13:12		
5	Proverbs 11.25	8	Jonah 4:11		

OTHER BOOKS BY THE SAME AUTHOR

Paths of Righteousness in Psalm 23
The Growing Pains of Peter
In Sickness and in Health
Dying is Living

All are obtainable from New Living Publishers
Web site: www.newlivingpublishers.co.uk